Lawful Permanent Resident Spouse Petitioning Spouse

Getting the Green Card by Marrying a Green Card Holder

Attorney Brian D. Lerner

BDL
LAW OFFICES OF
BRIAN D. LERNER
A PROFESSIONAL CORPORATION

ATTORNEY DRAFTED IMMIGRATION PETITIONS

By

Brian D. Lerner

Attorney at Law

Disclaimer and Terms of Use:

Effort has been made to ensure that the information in this book is accurate and complete. However, the author and the publisher do not warrant that this particular petition will mirror or be exactly as your situation. There has not been any attorney-client agreement created by the purchase of this petition or application. No legal advice has occurred. The cases, regulations and/or statutes cited may change at any time without notice.

ISBN: 978-1-958990-35-3

INTRODUCTION

There are a multitude of different immigration petitions and applications. They are complex and full of requirements. Obviously, it would be best to hire an immigration attorney to best prepare the petitions and applications. However, this can certainly cost thousands of dollars.

The next best option is to get a sample of the petition written by an experienced immigration attorney. The samples cost a fraction what would be charged by an immigration attorney. However, while the reader has to alter, amend and change the parts of the sample petition to reflect their actual situation, it is a fantastic roadmap for them to use. If the reader has purchased the entire petition or application, they will have real live samples of cover letters, forms, declarations, affidavits and the necessary exhibits to use. The samples come from real cases and the names of those clients have been redacted to protect the privacy of that person or corporation.

These are petitions and applications that have been drafted by an experienced immigration attorney with over 25 years of experience. Get the benefits of that experience without the costs.

CONTENTS

About the Law Offices of Brian D. Lerner

The Law Offices of Brian D. Lerner, APC. The law practice consists of Immigration and Nationality Law and everything involved with and regarding immigration which includes citizenship, investment visas, family and employment visas, removal and deportation hearings, appeals, waivers, adjustment, consulate processing and all types of immigration and citizenship matters. Thousands of families have been reunited and/or permitted to stay in the U.S. and/or return to the U.S. because of the successful work of Immigration Attorney Brian D. Lerner.

This law offices handles all types of immigration cases including family based and employment based. Immigration issues range from immigration court proceedings to trying to fix what paralegals may have done that was neither correct nor proper. Foreign nationals must have experience lawyers admitted to practice law.

The Law Offices of Brian D. Lerner, APC, handles cases arising from business visas, work permits, Green Cards, non-immigrant visas, deportation, citizenship, appeals and all areas of immigration. The Law Offices of Brian D. Lerner, APC does EB-5 Investor Visas, H-1B Specialty Occupation, L-1 Intracompany Transferee, E-2 Treaty Investor, E-1 Treaty Trader, O-1 Extraordinary Ability among others. Regarding immigrant visas for the Green Card, the firm does PERM and advanced degree PERM, Family Petitions, and Extraordinary Alien Petitions. In addition to affirmative petitions, the Law Firm represents people in people in deportation and removal hearings, including political asylum, withholding of removal, and convention against torture cases.

Brian D. Lerner has been certified as an expert in Immigration & Nationality Law by the California State Bar, Board of Legal Specialization since 2000 and has been re-certified three times. He now passes on his decades of experience by allowing the Reader, Law Schools, Professors and other Immigration Attorneys to purchase sample petitions on every facet of Immigration Law.

About the Lawful Permanent Resident Spouse Petitioning Spouse

Ready to Petition your Spouse? In this case, are you a Lawful Permanent Resident and you are petitioning your spouse, it will be considered a Second Preference Petition and you can move on to the next step the moment it becomes current to either adjusting status or consulate processing. The first part must be done and must be done properly in order to ever proceed to the next part. Without a proper I-130 application there will never be a Green Card. If approved, then you could move onto the next step in the Immigration process. If not approved, it will take years of red tape. Remember, it is your responsibility to submit everything correctly. This sample I-130 Petition has everything necessary to give you the best chance possible to get an approval. Just input your own information and use the application as a guide. It has been prepared by an expert Immigration Attorney. Thus, this book will allow you to see a guide of how it is done, prepared and submitted.

ATTORNEY COVER LETTER

Law Offices of Brian D. Lerner

A PROFESSIONAL CORPORATION

CERTIFIED SPECIALIST IN IMMIGRATION AND NATIONALITY LAW
ADMITTED TO THE U.S. SUPREME COURT

LONG BEACH, CALIFORNIA (562) 495-0554
CARSON, CALIFORNIA (310) 684-5420

October 22, 2018

U.S. Citizenship and Immigration Services
Attn: I-130
P.O. Box 804625
Chicago, IL 60680-4107

RE: I-130, Petition for Alien Relative
Petitioner: [redacted]
Beneficiary: [redacted]

Dear Sir/Madam:

We hereby submit an I-130, Petition of Alien Relative, for [redacted] (hereinafter "Petitioner") on behalf of his spouse, [redacted] (hereinafter "Beneficiary").

Enclosed herein please find the following documents:

FORMS

Form:	Description:
G-28	Notice of Entry of Appearance as Attorney or Accredited Representative (Petitioner);
I-130	Petition for Alien Relative with $535.00 Filing Fee; and
I-130A	Supplemental Information for Spouse Beneficiary.

We also enclose two passport-style photographs of the Petitioner and the Beneficiary.

EXHIBITS

Exhibits:	Description:
1.	Copy of Petitioner's Birth Certificate with English Translation;
2.	Copy of Petitioner's Legal Permanent Resident;
3.	Copy of Beneficiary's Birth Certificate with English Translation;

4. Copy of Beneficiary's Foreign Passport;
5. Copy of Petitioner's and Beneficiary's Marriage Certificate;
6. Family Photos of Petitioner and Beneficiary; and
7. Proof of Relationship Between the Petitioner and the Beneficiary.

Under the Immigration and Nationality Act ("INA") § 201(b)(2)(A)(i), the Immediate Relatives, including children, spouses and parents, of a U.S. citizen may be petitioned for an immigrant visa, without being subjected to direct numerical limitations. All other family sponsored preference catergories, includings spouses and children of lawful permanent residents, are subject to direct numerical limitations. See INA § 201(b)(2)(A)(i).

In the present case, Petitioner is a U.S. Permanent Resident. Petitioner and Beneficiary were married on January 10, 1996 in Atotonilcon El Grande, Hildalgo, Mexico. Therefore, Petitioner is qualified to file an Alien Relative Petition in behalf of his spouse, Beneficiary.

Based on the foregoing, we respectfully submit that the attached evidence shows the necessary relationship exists and that the instant I-130 should be approved.

Thank you for your consideration in this matter. Should you have any further questions, please feel free to contact our office at (562) 495-0554.

Sincerely,

Attorney at Law

FORMS

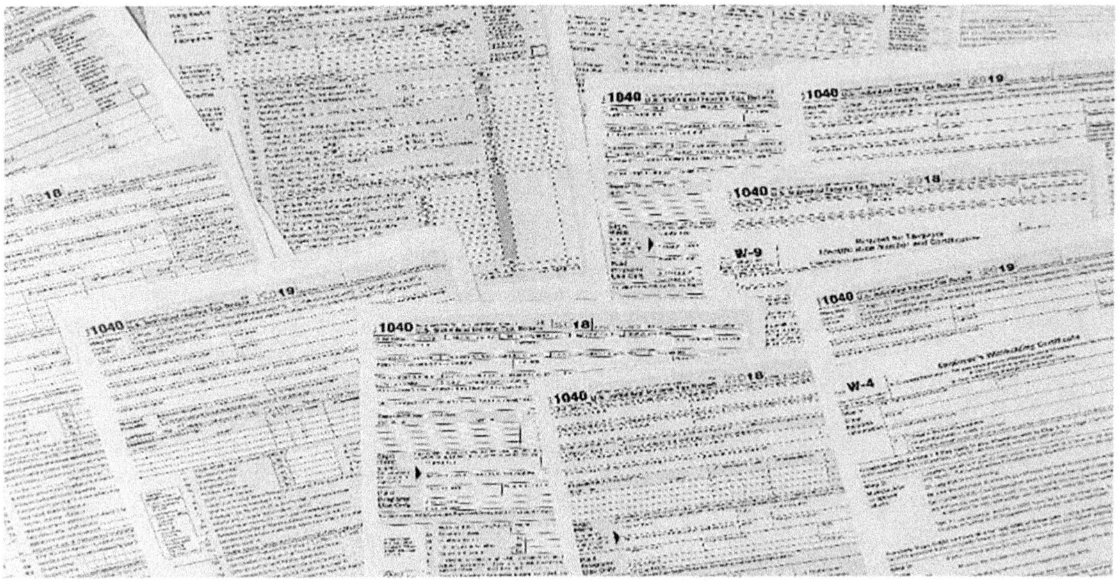

Notice of Entry of Appearance as Attorney or Accredited Representative

Department of Homeland Security

DHS Form G-28
OMB No. 1615-0105
Expires 05/31/2021

Part 1. Information About Attorney or Accredited Representative

1. USCIS Online Account Number (if any) ▶

Name of Attorney or Accredited Representative

2.a. Family Name (Last Name) [redacted]
2.b. Given Name (First Name) [redacted]
2.c. Middle Name [redacted]

Address of Attorney or Accredited Representative

3.a. Street Number and Name: 3233 E. Broadway
3.b. ☐ Apt. ☐ Ste. ☐ Flr.
3.c. City or Town: Long Beach
3.d. State: CA 3.e. ZIP Code: 90803
3.f. Province
3.g. Postal Code
3.h. Country: USA

Contact Information of Attorney or Accredited Representative

4. Daytime Telephone Number [redacted]
5. Mobile Telephone Number (if any)
6. Email Address (if any) [redacted]
7. Fax Number (if any) [redacted]

Part 2. Eligibility Information for Attorney or Accredited Representative

Select **all applicable** items.

1.a. ☒ I am an attorney eligible to practice law in, and a member in good standing of, the bar of the highest courts of the following states, possessions, territories, commonwealths, or the District of Columbia. If you need extra space to complete this section, use the space provided in **Part 6. Additional Information**.

Licensing Authority: California Supreme Court

1.b. Bar Number [redacted]

1.c. I (select **only one** box) ☒ am not ☐ am subject to any order suspending, enjoining, restraining, disbarring, or otherwise restricting me in the practice of law. If you are subject to any orders, use the space provided in **Part 6. Additional Information** to provide an explanation.

1.d. Name of Law Firm or Organization (if applicable): Law Offices of Brian D. Lerner, APC

2.a. ☐ I am an accredited representative of the following qualified nonprofit religious, charitable, social service, or similar organization established in the United States and recognized by the Department of Justice in accordance with 8 CFR part 1292.

2.b. Name of Recognized Organization

2.c. Date of Accreditation (mm/dd/yyyy)

3. ☐ I am associated with ____, the attorney or accredited representative of record who previously filed Form G-28 in this case, and my appearance as an attorney or accredited representative for a limited purpose is at his or her request.

4.a. ☐ I am a law student or law graduate working under the direct supervision of the attorney or accredited representative of record on this form in accordance with the requirements in 8 CFR 292.1(a)(2).

4.b. Name of Law Student or Law Graduate

Part 3. Notice of Appearance as Attorney or Accredited Representative

If you need extra space to complete this section, use the space provided in **Part 6. Additional Information**.

This appearance relates to immigration matters before (select **only one** box):

1.a. [X] U.S. Citizenship and Immigration Services (USCIS)

1.b. List the form numbers or specific matter in which appearance is entered.

I-130

2.a. [ ] U.S. Immigration and Customs Enforcement (ICE)

2.b. List the specific matter in which appearance is entered.

3.a. [ ] U.S. Customs and Border Protection (CBP)

3.b. List the specific matter in which appearance is entered.

4. Receipt Number (if any)

▶

5. I enter my appearance as an attorney or accredited representative at the request of the (select **only one** box):

[ ] Applicant [X] Petitioner [ ] Requestor

[ ] Beneficiary/Derivative [ ] Respondent (ICE, CBP)

Information About Client (Applicant, Petitioner, Requestor, Beneficiary or Derivative, Respondent, or Authorized Signatory for an Entity)

6.a. Family Name (Last Name)

6.b. Given Name (First Name)

6.c. Middle Name

7.a. Name of Entity (if applicable)

7.b. Title of Authorized Signatory for Entity (if applicable)

8. Client's USCIS Online Account Number (if any)

▶

9. Client's Alien Registration Number (A-Number) (if any)

▶ A-

Client's Contact Information

10. Daytime Telephone Number

11. Mobile Telephone Number (if any)

12. Email Address (if any)

Mailing Address of Client

NOTE: Provide the client's mailing address. **Do not** provide the business mailing address of the attorney or accredited representative **unless** it serves as the safe mailing address on the application or petition being filed with this Form G-28.

13.a. Street Number and Name

13.b. [ ] Apt. [ ] Ste. [ ] Flr.

13.c. City or Town

13.d. State CA **13.e.** ZIP Code

13.f. Province

13.g. Postal Code

13.h. Country

USA

Part 4. Client's Consent to Representation and Signature

Consent to Representation and Release of Information

I have requested the representation of and consented to being represented by the attorney or accredited representative named in **Part 1.** of this form. According to the Privacy Act of 1974 and U.S. Department of Homeland Security (DHS) policy, I also consent to the disclosure to the named attorney or accredited representative of any records pertaining to me that appear in any system of records of USCIS, ICE, or CBP.

Part 4. Client's Consent to Representation and Signature (continued)

Options Regarding Receipt of USCIS Notices and Documents

USCIS will send notices to both a represented party (the client) and his, her, or its attorney or accredited representative either through mail or electronic delivery. USCIS will send all secure identity documents and Travel Documents to the client's U.S. mailing address.

If you want to have notices and/or secure identity documents sent to your attorney or accredited representative of record rather than to you, please select **all applicable** items below. You may change these elections through written notice to USCIS.

1.a. [X] I request that USCIS send original notices on an application or petition to the U.S. business address of my attorney or accredited representative as listed in this form.

1.b. [ ] I request that USCIS send any secure identity document (Permanent Resident Card, Employment Authorization Document, or Travel Document) that I receive to the U.S. business address of my attorney or accredited representative (or to a designated military or diplomatic address in a foreign country (if permitted)).

NOTE: If your notice contains Form I-94, Arrival-Departure Record, USCIS will send the notice to the U.S. business address of your attorney or accredited representative. If you would rather have your Form I-94 sent directly to you, select **Item Number 1.c.**

1.c. [ ] I request that USCIS send my notice containing Form I-94 to me at my U.S. mailing address.

Signature of Client or Authorized Signatory for an Entity

2.a. Signature of Client or Authorized Signatory for an Entity

2.b. Date of Signature (mm/dd/yyyy) 10/22/2018

Part 5. Signature of Attorney or Accredited Representative

I have read and understand the regulations and conditions contained in 8 CFR 103.2 and 292 governing appearances and representation before DHS. I declare under penalty of perjury under the laws of the United States that the information I have provided on this form is true and correct.

1.a. Signature of Attorney or Accredited Representative

1.b. Date of Signature (mm/dd/yyyy) 10/22/18

2.a. Signature of Law Student or Law Graduate

2.b. Date of Signature (mm/dd/yyyy)

Part 6. Additional Information

If you need extra space to provide any additional information within this form, use the space below. If you need more space than what is provided, you may make copies of this page to complete and file with this form or attach a separate sheet of paper. Type or print your name at the top of each sheet; indicate the **Page Number**, **Part Number**, and **Item Number** to which your answer refers; and sign and date each sheet.

1.a Family Name (Last Name) [redacted]

1.b. Given Name (First Name) [redacted]

1.c. Middle Name

2.a. Page Number **2.b.** Part Number **2.c.** Item Number

2.d.

3.a. Page Number **3.b.** Part Number **3.c.** Item Number

3.d.

4.a. Page Number **4.b.** Part Number **4.c.** Item Number

4.d.

5.a. Page Number **5.b.** Part Number **5.c.** Item Number

5.d.

6.a. Page Number **6.b.** Part Number **6.c.** Item Number

6.d.

Petition for Alien Relative

Department of Homeland Security
U.S. Citizenship and Immigration Services

USCIS
Form I-130
OMB No. 1615-0012
Expires 07/31/2018

For USCIS Use Only		Fee Stamp	Action Stamp
A-Number: A-			
Initial Receipt			
Resubmitted			
Relocated	Section of Law/Visa Category		
Received	[ ] 201(b) Spouse - IR-1/CR-1 [ ] 203(a)(1) Unm. S/D - F1-1 [ ] 203(a)(2)(B) Unm. S/D - F2-4		
Sent	[ ] 201(b) Child - IR-2/CR-2 [ ] 203(a)(2)(A) Spouse - F2-1 [ ] 203(a)(3) Married S/D - F3-1		
Completed	[ ] 201(b) Parent - IR-5 [ ] 203(a)(2)(A) Child - F2-2 [ ] 203(a)(4) Brother/Sister - F4-1		
Approved	Petition was filed on (Priority Date mm/dd/yyyy):	[ ] Field Investigation [ ] Previously Forwarded [ ] 203(g) Resolved	[ ] Personal Interview [ ] Pet. A-File Reviewed [ ] Ben. A-File Reviewed [ ] 204(a)(2)(A) Resolved [ ] I-485 Filed Simultaneously [ ] 204(g) Resolved
Returned	PDR request granted/denied - New priority date (mm/dd/yyyy):		
Remarks			

At which USCIS office (e.g., NBC, VSC, LOS, CRO) was Form I-130 adjudicated? ______

To be completed by an attorney or accredited representative (if any).			
[X] Select this box if Form G-28 is attached.	Volag Number (if any)	Attorney State Bar Number (if applicable)	Attorney or Accredited Representative USCIS Online Account Number (if any)

► **START HERE - Type or print in black ink.**

If you need extra space to complete any section of this petition, use the space provided in **Part 9. Additional Information. Complete and submit as many copies of Part 9., as necessary, with your petition.**

Part 1. Relationship (You are the Petitioner. Your relative is the Beneficiary)

1. I am filing this petition for my (Select **only one** box):
   [X] Spouse [ ] Parent [ ] Brother/Sister [ ] Child
2. If you are filing this petition for your child or parent, select the box that describes your relationship (Select **only** one box):
   [ ] Child was born to parents who were married to each other at the time of the child's birth
   [ ] Stepchild/Stepparent
   [ ] Child was born to parents who were not married to each other at the time of the child's birth
   [ ] Child was adopted (not an Orphan or Hague Convention adoptee)
3. If the beneficiary is your brother/sister, are you related by adoption? [ ] Yes [X] No
4. Did you gain lawful permanent resident status or citizenship through adoption? [ ] Yes [X] No

Part 2. Information About You (Petitioner)

1. Alien Registration Number (A-Number) (if any)
2. USCIS Online Account Number (if any) ►
3. U.S. Social Security Number ►

Your Full Name

4.a. Family Name (Last Name)
4.b. Given Name (First Name)
4.c. Middle Name

Part 2. Information About You (Petitioner) (continued)

Other Names Used (if any)

Provide all other names you have ever used, including aliases, maiden name, and nicknames.

5.a. Family Name (Last Name) None

5.b. Given Name (First Name)

5.c. Middle Name

Other Information

6. City/Town/Village of Birth

7. Country of Birth

Mexico

8. Date of Birth (mm/dd/yyyy) 01/19/1965

9. Sex ☒ Male ☐ Female

Mailing Address

10.a. In Care Of Name

10.b. Street Number and Name

10.c. ☐ Apt. ☐ Ste. ☐ Flr.

10.d. City or Town

10.e. State CA **10.f.** ZIP Code

10.g. Province

10.h. Postal Code

10.i. Country

USA

11. Is your current mailing address the same as your physical address? ☒ Yes ☐ No

If you answered "No" to **Item Number 11.**, provide information on your physical address in **Item Numbers 12.a. - 13.b.**

Address History

Provide your physical addresses for the last five years, whether inside or outside the United States. Provide your current address first if it is different from your mailing address in **Item Numbers 10.a. - 10.i.**

Physical Address 1

12.a. Street Number and Name

12.b. ☐ Apt. ☐ Ste. ☐ Flr.

12.c. City or Town

12.d. State **12.e.** ZIP Code

12.f. Province

12.g. Postal Code

12.h. Country

13.a. Date From (mm/dd/yyyy)

13.b. Date To (mm/dd/yyyy) PRESENT

Physical Address 2

14.a. Street Number and Name

14.b. ☐ Apt. ☐ Ste. ☐ Flr.

14.c. City or Town

14.d. State CA **14.e.** ZIP Code

14.f. Province

14.g. Postal Code

14.h. Country

USA

15.a. Date From (mm/dd/yyyy) 01/01/2012

15.b. Date To (mm/dd/yyyy) 11/01/2016

Your Marital Information

16. How many times have you been married? ▶ 1

17. Current Marital Status

☐ Single, Never Married ☒ Married ☐ Divorced ☐ Widowed ☐ Separated ☐ Annulled

Part 2. Information About You (Petitioner) (continued)

18. Date of Current Marriage (if currently married) (mm/dd/yyyy) 01/10/1996

Place of Your Current Marriage (if married)

19.a. City or Town [redacted]

19.b. State

19.c. Province [redacted]

19.d. [redacted]

Names of All Your Spouses (if any)

Provide information on your current spouse (if currently married) first and then list all your prior spouses (if any).

Spouse 1

20.a. Family Name (Last Name) [redacted]

20.b. Given Name (First Name) [redacted]

20.c. Middle Name [redacted]

21. Date Marriage Ended (mm/dd/yyyy)

Spouse 2

22.a. Family Name (Last Name)

22.b. Given Name (First Name)

22.c. Middle Name

23. Date Marriage Ended (mm/dd/yyyy)

Information About Your Parents

Parent 1's Information

Full Name of Parent 1

24.a. Family Name (Last Name) [redacted]

24.b. Given Name (First Name) [redacted]

24.c. Middle Name

25. Date of Birth (mm/dd/yyyy) 01/18/1946

26. Sex ☒ Male ☐ Female

27. Country of Birth
Mexico

28. City/Town/Village of Residence
Pachuca

29. Country of Residence
Mexico

Parent 2's Information

Full Name of Parent 2

30.a. Family Name (Last Name) [redacted]

30.b. Given Name (First Name) [redacted]

30.c. Middle Name

31. Date of Birth (mm/dd/yyyy) 10/27/1948

32. Sex ☐ Male ☒ Female

33. Country of Birth
Mexico

34. City/Town/Village of Residence
Pachuca

35. Country of Residence
Mexico

Additional Information About You (Petitioner)

36. I am a (Select **only one** box):
☐ U.S. Citizen ☒ Lawful Permanent Resident

If you are a U.S. citizen, complete Item Number 37.

37. My citizenship was acquired through (Select **only one** box):
☐ Birth in the United States
☐ Naturalization
☐ Parents

38. Have you obtained a Certificate of Naturalization or a Certificate of Citizenship? ☐ Yes ☒ No

If you answered "Yes" to **Item Number 38.**, complete the following:

39.a. Certificate Number

39.b. Place of Issuance

39.c. Date of Issuance (mm/dd/yyyy)

Part 2. Information About You (Petitioner) (continued)

If you are a lawful permanent resident, complete **Item Numbers 40.a. - 41.**

40.a. Class of Admission: S26

40.b. Date of Admission (mm/dd/yyyy): 12/01/1990

Place of Admission

40.c. City or Town: Los Angeles

40.d State: CA

41. Did you gain lawful permanent resident status through marriage to a U.S. citizen or lawful permanent resident?
☐ Yes ☒ No

Employment History

Provide your employment history for the last five years, whether inside or outside the United States. Provide your current employment first. If you are currently unemployed, type or print "Unemployed" in **Item Number 42.**

Employer 1

42. Name of Employer/Company: [redacted]

43.a. Street Number and Name: [redacted]

43.b. ☐ Apt. ☒ Ste. ☐ Flr. 110

43.c. City or Town: [redacted]

43.d. State: CA **43.e.** ZIP Code: [redacted]

43.f. Province:

43.g. Postal Code:

43.h. Country: USA

44. Your Occupation: [redacted]

45.a. Date From (mm/dd/yyyy): 11/01/2016

45.b. Date To (mm/dd/yyyy): PRESENT

Employer 2

46. Name of Employer/Company: [redacted]

47.a. Street Number and Name: [redacted]

47.b. ☐ Apt. ☐ Ste. ☐ Flr.

47.c. City or Town: [redacted]

47.d. State: CA **47.e.** ZIP Code: [redacted]

47.f. Province:

47.g. Postal Code:

47.h. Country: USA

48. Your Occupation: [redacted]

49.a. Date From (mm/dd/yyyy): 05/01/2016

49.b. Date To (mm/dd/yyyy): 11/01/2016

Part 3. Biographic Information

NOTE: Provide the biographic information about you, the petitioner.

1. Ethnicity (Select **only one** box)
☒ Hispanic or Latino
☐ Not Hispanic or Latino

2. Race (Select **all applicable** boxes)
☒ White
☐ Asian
☐ Black or African American
☐ American Indian or Alaska Native
☐ Native Hawaiian or Other Pacific Islander

3. Height Feet 5 Inches 5

4. Weight Pounds 1 3 0

5. Eye Color (Select **only one** box)
☐ Black ☐ Blue ☒ Brown
☐ Gray ☐ Green ☐ Hazel
☐ Maroon ☐ Pink ☐ Unknown/Other

Part 3. Biographic Information (continued)

6. Hair Color (Select **only** one box)

- [ ] Bald (No hair) [ ] Black [ ] Blond
- [x] Brown [ ] Gray [ ] Red
- [ ] Sandy [ ] White [ ] Unknown/Other

Part 4. Information About Beneficiary

1. Alien Registration Number (A-Number) (if any) ▶ A-

2. USCIS Online Account Number (if any) ▶

3. U.S. Social Security Number (if any) ▶

Beneficiary's Full Name

4.a. Family Name (Last Name) [redacted]

4.b. Given Name (First Name) [redacted]

4.c. Middle Name [redacted]

Other Names Used (if any)

Provide all other names the beneficiary has ever used, including aliases, maiden name, and nicknames.

5.a. Family Name (Last Name) None

5.b. Given Name (First Name)

5.c. Middle Name

Other Information About Beneficiary

6. City/Town/Village of Birth [redacted]

7. Country of Birth Mexico

8. Date of Birth (mm/dd/yyyy) 01/03/1978

9. Sex [ ] Male [x] Female

10. Has anyone else ever filed a petition for the beneficiary? [ ] Yes [x] No [ ] Unknown

NOTE: Select "Unknown" *only* if you do not know, and the beneficiary also does not know, if anyone else has ever filed a petition for the beneficiary.

Beneficiary's Physical Address

If the beneficiary lives outside the United States in a home without a street number or name, leave **Item Numbers 11.a.** and **11.b.** blank.

11.a. Street Number and Name [redacted]

11.b. [ ] Apt. [ ] Ste. [ ] Flr.

11.c. City or Town [redacted]a

11.d. State 11.e. ZIP Code

11.f. Province [redacted]

11.g. Postal Code [redacted]

11.h. Country Mexico

Other Address and Contact Information

Provide the address in the United States where the beneficiary intends to live, if different from **Item Numbers 11.a. - 11.h.** If the address is the same, type or print "SAME" in **Item Number 12.a.**

12.a Street Number and Name [redacted]

12.b. [ ] Apt. [ ] Ste. [ ] Flr.

12.c. City or Town [redacted]

12.d. State CA 12.e. ZIP Code [redacted]

Provide the beneficiary's address outsid[redacted]e United States, if different from **Item Numbers 11.a. - 11.h.** If the address is the same, type or print "SAME" in **Item Number 13.a.**

13.a. Street Number and Name SAME

13.b. [ ] Apt. [ ] Ste. [ ] Flr.

13.c. City or Town

13.d. Province

13.e. Postal Code

13.f. Country

14. Daytime Telephone Number (if any) [redacted]

Part 4. Information About Beneficiary (continued)

15. Mobile Telephone Number (if any)

16. E[redacted]ny

Beneficiary's Marital Information

17. How many times has the beneficiary been married? ▶ 1

18. Current Marital Status

☐ Single, Never Married ☒ Married ☐ Divorced ☐ Widowed ☐ Separated ☐ Annulled

19. Date of Current Marriage (if currently married) (mm/dd/yyyy) 01/10/1996

Place of Beneficiary's Current Marriage (if married)

20.a. City or Town Atotonilcoel Grande

20.b. State

20.c. Province

20.d. Country Mexico

Names of Beneficiary's Spouses (if any)

Provide information on the beneficiary's current spouse (if currently married) first and then list all the beneficiary's prior spouses (if any).

Spouse 1

21.a. Family Name (Last Name)

21.b. Given Name (First Name) Marti n

21.c. Middle Name

22. Date Marriage Ended (mm/dd/yyyy)

Spouse 2

23.a. Family Name (Last Name)

23.b. Given Name (First Name)

23.c. Middle Name

24. Date Marriage Ended (mm/dd/yyyy)

Information About Beneficiary's Family

Provide information about the beneficiary's spouse and children.

Person 1

25.a. Family Name (Last Name)

25.b. Given Name (First Name)

25.c. Middle Name

26. Relationship Spouse

27. Date of Birth (mm/dd/yyyy)

28. Country of Birth

Person 2

29.a. Family Name (Last Name)

29.b. Given Name (First Name)

29.c. Middle Name

30. Relationship

31. Date of Birth (mm/dd/yyyy) 06/16/1997

32. Country of Birth Mexico

Person 3

33.a. Family Name (Last Name)

33.b. Given Name (First Name)

33.c. Middle Name

34. Relationship

35. Date of Birth (mm/dd/yyyy) 11/06/2001

36. Country of Birth Mexico

Part 4. Information About Beneficiary (continued)

Person 4

37.a. Family Name (Last Name) [redacted]

37.b. Given Name (First Name) [redacted]

37.c. Middle Name

38. Relationship [redacted]

39. Date of Birth (mm/dd/yyyy) 12/18/2002

40. Country of Birth [redacted]

Person 5

41.a. Family Name (Last Name)

41.b. Given Name (First Name)

41.c. Middle Name

42. Relationship

43. Date of Birth (mm/dd/yyyy)

44. Country of Birth

Beneficiary's Entry Information

45. Was the beneficiary EVER in the United States?

☐ Yes ☒ No

If the beneficiary is currently in the United States, complete **Items Numbers 46.a. - 46.d.**

46.a. He or she arrived as a (Class of Admission):

46.b. Form I-94 Arrival-Departure Record Number

▶

46.c. Date of Arrival (mm/dd/yyyy)

46.d. Date authorized stay expired, or will expire, as shown on Form I-94 or Form I-95 (mm/dd/yyyy) or type or print "D/S" for Duration of Status

47. Passport Number [redacted]

48. Travel Document Number

49. Country of Issuance for Passport or Travel Document [redacted]

50. Expiration Date for Passport or Travel Document (mm/dd/yyyy) 08/31/2021

Beneficiary's Employment Information

Provide the beneficiary's current employment information (if applicable), even if they are employed outside of the United States. If the beneficiary is currently unemployed, type or print "Unemployed" in **Item Number 51.a.**

51.a. Name of Current Employer (if applicable) [redacted]

51.b. Street Number and Name

51.c. ☐ Apt. ☐ Ste. ☐ Flr.

51.d. City or Town

51.e. State **51.f.** ZIP Code

51.g. Province

51.h. Postal Code

51.i. Country

52. Date Employment Began (mm/dd/yyyy)

Additional Information About Beneficiary

53. Was the beneficiary EVER in immigration proceedings?

☐ Yes ☒ No

54. If you answered "Yes," select the type of proceedings and provide the location and date of the proceedings.

☐ Removal ☐ Exclusion/Deportation

☐ Rescission ☐ Other Judicial Proceedings

55.a. City or Town

55.b. State

56. Date (mm/dd/yyyy)

Part 4. Information About Beneficiary (continued)

If the beneficiary's native written language does not use Roman letters, type or print his or her name and foreign address in their native written language.

57.a. Family Name (Last Name)

57.b. Given Name (First Name)

57.c. Middle Name

58.a. Street Number and Name

58.b. ☐ Apt. ☐ Ste. ☐ Flr.

58.c. City or Town

58.d. Province

58.e. Postal Code

58.f. Country

If filing for your spouse, provide the last address at which you physically lived together. If you never lived together, type or print, "Never lived together" in Item Number 59.a.

59.a. Street Number and Name [redacted]

59.b. ☐ Apt. ☐ Ste. ☐ Flr.

59.c. City or Town [redacted]

59.d. State 59.e. ZIP Code

59.f. Province [redacted]

59.g. Postal Code [redacted]

59.h. Country Mexico

60.a. Date From (mm/dd/yyyy) 08/01/1996

60.b. Date To (mm/dd/yyyy) 00/00/1997

The beneficiary is in the United States and will apply for adjustment of status to that of a lawful permanent resident at the U.S. Citizenship and Immigration Services (USCIS) office in:

61.a. City or Town

61.b. State

The beneficiary will not apply for adjustment of status in the United States, but he or she will apply for an immigrant visa abroad at the U.S. Embassy or U.S. Consulate in:

62.a. City or Town [redacted]

62.b. Province [redacted]

62.c. Country [redacted]

NOTE: Choosing a U.S. Embassy or U.S. Consulate outside the country of the beneficiary's last residence does not guarantee that it will accept the beneficiary's case for processing. In these situations, the designated U.S. Embassy or U.S. Consulate has discretion over whether or not to accept the beneficiary's case.

Part 5. Other Information

1. Have you EVER previously filed a petition for this beneficiary or any other alien? ☒ Yes ☐ No

If you answered "Yes," provide the name, place, date of filing, and the result.

2.a. Family Name (Last Name) [redacted]

2.b. Given Name (First Name) [redacted]

2.c. Middle Name [redacted]n

3.a. City or Town Los Angeles

3.b. State CA

4. Date Filed (mm/dd/yyyy) 10/01/2018

5. Result (for example, approved, denied, withdrawn) [redacted]

If you are also submitting separate petitions for other relatives, provide the names of and your relationship to each relative.

Relative 1

6.a. Family Name (Last Name) [redacted]

6.b. Given Name (First Name) [redacted]

6.c. Middle Name

7. Relationship [redacted]

Part 5. Other Information (continued)

Relative 2

8.a. Family Name (Last Name) [redacted]

8.b. Given Name (First Name) E[redacted]

8.c. Middle Name

9. Relationship [redacted]

WARNING: USCIS investigates the claimed relationships and verifies the validity of documents you submit. If you falsify a family relationship to obtain a visa, USCIS may seek to have you criminally prosecuted.

PENALTIES: By law, you may be imprisoned for up to 5 years or fined $250,000, or both, for entering into a marriage contract in order to evade any U.S. immigration law. In addition, you may be fined up to $10,000 and imprisoned for up to 5 years, or both, for knowingly and willfully falsifying or concealing a material fact or using any false document in submitting this petition.

Part 6. Petitioner's Statement, Contact Information, Declaration, and Signature

NOTE: Read the **Penalties** section of the Form I-130 Instructions before completing this part.

Petitioner's Statement

NOTE: Select the box for either **Item Number 1.a.** or **1.b.** If applicable, select the box for **Item Number 2.**

1.a. ☐ I can read and understand English, and I have read and understand every question and instruction on this petition and my answer to every question.

1.b. ☒ The interpreter named in **Part 7.** read to me every question and instruction on this petition and my answer to every question in

Spanish

a language in which I am fluent. I understood all of this information as interpreted.

2. ☒ A [redacted] named in **Part 8.**, [redacted] based only upon information I provided or authorized.

Petitioner's Contact Information

3. Petitioner's Daytime Telephone Number [redacted]

4. Petitioner's Mobile Telephone Number (if any) [redacted]

5. Petitioner's Email Address (if any)

Petitioner's Declaration and Certification

Copies of any documents I have submitted are exact photocopies of unaltered, original documents, and I understand that USCIS may require that I submit original documents to USCIS at a later date. Furthermore, I authorize the release of any information from any of my records that USCIS may need to determine my eligibility for the immigration benefit I seek.

I further authorize release of information contained in this petition, in supporting documents, and in my USCIS records to other entities and persons where necessary for the administration and enforcement of U.S. immigration laws.

I understand that USCIS may require me to appear for an appointment to take my biometrics (fingerprints, photograph, and/or signature) and, at that time, if I am required to provide biometrics, I will be required to sign an oath reaffirming that:

1) I provided or authorized all of the information contained in, and submitted with, my petition;

2) I reviewed and understood all of the information in, and submitted with, my petition; and

3) All of this information was complete, true, and correct at the time of filing.

I certify, under penalty of perjury, that all of the information in my petition and any document submitted with it were provided or authorized by me, that I reviewed and understand all of the information contained in, and submitted with, my petition, and that all of this information is complete, true, and correct.

Petitioner's Signature

6.a. Petitioner's Signature (sign in ink)

➡ [redacted]

6.b. Date of Signature (mm/dd/yyyy) 10/22/2018

NOTE TO ALL PETITIONERS: If you do not completely fill out this petition or fail to submit required documents listed in the Instructions, USCIS may deny your petition.

Part 7. Interpreter's Contact Information, Certification, and Signature

Provide the following information about the interpreter if you used one.

Interpreter's Full Name

1.a. Interpreter's Family Name (Last Name)

1.b. Interpreter's Given Name (First Name)

2. Interpreter's Business or Organization Name (if any)
Law Offices of Brian D. Lerner, APC

Interpreter's Mailing Address

3.a. Street Number and Name: 3233 E. Broadway

3.b. ☐ Apt. ☐ Ste. ☐ Flr.

3.c. City or Town: Long Beach

3.d. State: CA 3.e. ZIP Code: 90806

3.f. Province

3.g. Postal Code

3.h. Country
USA

Interpreter's Contact Information

4. Interpreter's Daytime Telephone Number

5. Interpreter's Mobile Telephone Number (if any)

6. Interpreter's Email Address (if any)

Interpreter's Certification

I certify, under penalty of perjury, that:

I am fluent in English and Spanish, which is the same language provided in **Part 6., Item Number 1.b.**, and I have read to this petitioner in the identified language every question and instruction on this petition and his or her answer to every question. The petitioner informed me that he or she understands every instruction, question, and answer on the petition, including the **Petitioner's Declaration and Certification**, and has verified the accuracy of every answer.

Interpreter's Signature

7.a. Interpreter's Signature (sign in ink)

7.b. Date of Signature (mm/dd/yyyy) 10/22/18

Part 8. Contact Information, Declaration, and Signature of the Person Preparing this Petition, if Other Than the Petitioner

Provide the following information about the preparer.

Preparer's Full Name

1.a. Preparer's Family Name (Last Name)

1.b. Preparer's Given Name (First Name)

2. Preparer's Business or Organization Name (if any)
Law Offices of Brian D. Lerner, APC

Preparer's Mailing Address

3.a. Street Number and Name: 3233 E. Broadway

3.b. ☐ Apt. ☐ Ste. ☐ Flr.

3.c. City or Town: Long Beach

3.d. State: CA 3.e. ZIP Code:

3.f. Province

3.g. Postal Code

3.h. Country
USA

Part 8. Contact Information, Declaration, and Signature of the Person Preparing this Petition, if Other Than the Petitioner (continued)

Preparer's Contact Information

4. Preparer's Daytime Telephone Number

5. Preparer's Mobile Telephone Number (if any)

6. Preparer's Email Address (if any)

Preparer's Statement

7.a. ☐ I am not an attorney or accredited representative but have prepared this petition on behalf of the petitioner and with the petitioner's consent.

7.b. ☒ I am an attorney or accredited representative and my representation of the petitioner in this case ☒ extends ☐ does not extend beyond the preparation of this petition.

NOTE: If you are an attorney or accredited representative whose representation extends beyond preparation of this petition, you may be obliged to submit a completed Form G-28, Notice of Entry of Appearance as Attorney or Accredited Representative, with this petition.

Preparer's Certification

By my signature, I certify, under penalty of perjury, that I prepared this petition at the request of the petitioner. The petitioner then reviewed this completed petition and informed me that he or she understands all of the information contained in, and submitted with, his or her petition, including the **Petitioner's Declaration and Certification**, and that all of this information is complete, true, and correct. I completed this petition based only on information that the petitioner provided to me or authorized me to obtain or use.

Preparer's Signature

8.a. Preparer's Signature (sign in ink)

8.b. Date of Signature (mm/dd/yyyy) 10/22/18

Part 9. Additional Information

If you need extra space to provide any additional information within this petition, use the space below. If you need more space than what is provided, you may make copies of this page to complete and file with this petition or attach a separate sheet of paper. Type or print your name and A-Number (if any) at the top of each sheet; indicate the **Page Number**, **Part Number**, and **Item Number** to which your answer refers; and sign and date each sheet.

1.a. Family Name (Last Name) [redacted]

1.b. Given Name (First Name)

1.c. Middle Name

2. A-Number (if any) ► A- [redacted]

3.a. Page Number **3.b.** Part Number **3.c.** Item Number

3.d.

4.a. Page Number **4.b.** Part Number **4.c.** Item Number

4.d.

5.a. Page Number **5.b.** Part Number **5.c.** Item Number

5.d.

6.a. Page Number **6.b.** Part Number **6.c.** Item Number

6.d.

7.a. Page Number **7.b.** Part Number **7.c.** Item Number

7.d.

Addendum

Form: I-130 (Page 1)

Part 2.: Additional Employment History of Petitioner:

Employer:
Address: P.O. Box 710, Pinole, CA, 94564, USA
Type of Work: Horse Groomer
Period: 01/01/2015 - 05/01/2016
Employer:
Address: 6616 E. Mountain View Road, Scottdale, AZ, 85253, USA
Type of Work: Horse Groomer
Period: 01/01/2012 - 01/01/2015

Supplemental Information for Spouse Beneficiary

Department of Homeland Security
U.S. Citizenship and Immigration Services

USCIS
Form I-130A
OMB No. 1615-0012
Expires 07/31/2018

To be completed by an attorney or accredited representative (if any).			
☒ Select this box if Form G-28 is attached.	Volag Number (if any)	Attorney State Bar Number (if applicable) [redacted]	Attorney or Accredited Representative USCIS Online Account Number (if any)

► **START HERE - Type or print in black ink.**

The purpose of this form is to collect additional information for a spouse beneficiary of Form I-130, Petition for Alien Relative. If your spouse is a U.S. citizen, lawful permanent resident, or non-citizen U.S. national who is filing Form I-130 on your behalf, you must complete and sign Form I-130A, Supplemental Information for Spouse Beneficiary, and submit it with the Form I-130 filed by your spouse. If you reside overseas, you still must complete Form I-130A, but you do not need to sign the form.

Part 1. Information About You (Spouse Beneficiary)

1. Alien Registration Number (A-Number) (if any) ► A-

2. USCIS Online Account Number (if any) ►

Your Full Name

3.a. Family Name (Last Name) [redacted]

3.b. Given Name (First Name) [redacted]

3.c. Middle Name [redacted]

Address History

Provide your physical addresses for the last five years, whether inside or outside the United States. Provide your current address first. If you need extra space to complete this section, use the space provided in **Part 7. Additional Information**.

Physical Address 1

4.a. Street Number and Name [redacted]

4.b. ☐ Apt. ☐ Ste. ☐ Flr.

4.c. City or Town [redacted]

4.d. State 4.e. ZIP Code

4.f. Province [redacted]

4.g. Postal Code [redacted]

4.h. Country Mexico

5.a. Date From (mm/dd/yyyy) 08/01/1996

5.b. Date To (mm/dd/yyyy) PRESENT

Physical Address 2

6.a. Street Number and Name

6.b. ☐ Apt. ☐ Ste. ☐ Flr.

6.c. City or Town

6.d. State 6.e. ZIP Code

6.f. Province

6.g. Postal Code

6.h. Country

7.a. Date From (mm/dd/yyyy)

7.b. Date To (mm/dd/yyyy)

Last Physical Address Outside the United States

Provide your last address outside the United States of more than one year (even if listed above).

8.a. Street Number and Name [redacted]

8.b. ☐ Apt. ☐ Ste. ☐ Flr.

8.c. City or Town [redacted]

8.d. Province [redacted]

8.e. Postal Code [redacted]

8.f. Country Mexico

Part 1. Information About You (The Spouse Beneficiary)

9.a. Date From (mm/dd/yyyy) 08/01/1996

9.b. Date To (mm/dd/yyyy) Present

Information About Parent 1

Full Name of Parent 1

10.a. Family Name (Maiden Name) [redacted]

10.b. Given Name (First Name) [redacted]

10.c. Middle Name

11. Date of Birth (mm/dd/yyyy) 03/11/1935

12. Sex ☐ Male ☒ Female

13. City/Town/Village of Birth [redacted]

14. Country of Birth Mexico

15. City/Town/Village of Residence [redacted]

16. Country of Residence Mexico

Information About Parent 2

Full Name of Parent 2

17.a. Family Name (Last Name) [redacted]

17.b. Given Name (First Name) [redacted]

17.c. Middle Name

18. Date of Birth (mm/dd/yyyy) 01/15/1923

19. Sex ☒ Male ☐ Female

20. City/Town/Village of Birth [redacted]

21. Country of Birth Mexico

22. City/Town/Village of Residence Deceased

23. Country of Residence Deceased

Part 2. Information About Your Employment

Provide your employment history for the last five years, whether inside or outside the United States. Provide your current employment first. If you are currently unemployed, type or print "Unemployed" in **Item Number 1.** below. If you need extra space to complete this section, use the space provided in **Part 7. Additional Information**.

Employment History

Employer 1

1. Name of Employer/Company Unemployed

2.a. Street Number and Name

2.b. ☐ Apt. ☐ Ste. ☐ Flr.

2.c. City or Town

2.d. State 2.e. ZIP Code

2.f. Province

2.g. Postal Code

2.h. Country

3. Your Occupation Unemployed

4.a. Date From (mm/dd/yyyy)

4.b. Date To (mm/dd/yyyy) PRESENT

Employer 2

5. Name of Employer/Company

6.a. Street Number and Name

6.b. ☐ Apt. ☐ Ste. ☐ Flr.

6.c. City or Town

6.d. State 6.e. ZIP Code

6.f. Province

6.g. Postal Code

6.h. Country

Part 2. Information About Your Employment (continued)

7. Your Occupation

8.a. Date From (mm/dd/yyyy)

8.b. Date To (mm/dd/yyyy)

Part 3. Information About Your Employment Outside the United States

Provide your last occupation outside the United States if not shown above. If you never worked outside the United States, provide this information in the space provided in **Part 7. Additional Information.**

1. Name of Employer/Company

Unemployed

2.a. Street Number and Name

2.b. ☐ Apt. ☐ Ste. ☐ Flr.

2.c. City or Town

2.d. State 2.e. ZIP Code

2.f. Province

2.g. Postal Code

2.h. Country

3. Your Occupation

4.a. Date From (mm/dd/yyyy)

4.b. Date To (mm/dd/yyyy)

Part 4. Spouse Beneficiary's Statement, Contact Information, Certification, and Signature

NOTE: Read the **Penalties** section of the Form I-130 and Form I-130A Instructions before completing this part.

Spouse Beneficiary's Statement

NOTE: Select the box for either **Item Number 1.a.** or **1.b.** If applicable, select the box for **Item Number 2.**

1.a. ☐ I can read and understand English, and I have read and understand every question and instruction on this form and my answer to every question.

1.b. ☒ The interpreter named in **Part 5.** read to me every question and instruction on this form and my answer to every question in

Spanish,

a language in which I am fluent, and I understood everything.

2. ☒ At my request, the preparer name in **Part 6.**,

[redacted],

prepared this form for me based only upon information I provided or authorized.

Spouse Beneficiary's Contact Information

3. Spouse Beneficiary's Daytime Telephone Number

4. Spouse Beneficiary's Mobile Telephone Number (if any)

5. Spouse Beneficiary's Email Address (if any)

[redacted]gmail.com

Spouse Beneficiary's Certification

Copies of any documents I have submitted are exact photocopies of unaltered, original documents, and I understand that USCIS may require that I submit original documents to USCIS at a later date. Furthermore, I authorize the release of any information from any of my records that USCIS may need to determine my eligibility for the immigration benefit I seek.

I further authorize release of information contained in this form, in supporting documents, and in my USCIS records to other entities and persons where necessary for the administration and enforcement of U.S. immigration laws.

I certify, under penalty of perjury, that I provided or authorized all of the information in this form, I understand all of the information contained in, and submitted with, my form, and that all of this information is complete, true, and correct.

Spouse Beneficiary's Signature

6.a. Spouse Beneficiary's Signature

6.b. Date of Signature (mm/dd/yyyy)

NOTE TO ALL SPOUSE BENEFICIARIES: If you do not completely fill out this form or fail to submit required documents listed in the Instructions, USCIS may deny the Form I-130 filed on your behalf.

Part 5. Interpreter's Contact Information, Certification, and Signature

Provide the following information about the interpreter you used to complete Form I-130A if he or she is different from the interpreter used to complete the Form I-130 filed on your behalf.

Interpreter's Full Name

1.a. Interpreter's Family Name (Last Name) [redacted]

1.b. Interpreter's Given Name (First Name) [redacted]

2. Interpreter's Business or Organization Name (if any) Law Offices of Brian D. Lerner, APC

Interpreter's Mailing Address

3.a. Street Number and Name 3233 E. Broadway

3.b. ☐ Apt. ☐ Ste. ☐ Flr.

3.c. City or Town Long Beach

3.d. State CA 3.e. ZIP Code 90803

3.f. Province

3.g. Postal Code

3.h. Country USA

Interpreter's Contact Information

4. Interpreter's Daytime Telephone Number [redacted]

5. Interpreter's Mobile Telephone Number (if any)

6. Interpreter's Email Address (if any) [redacted]

Interpreter's Certification

I certify, under penalty of perjury, that:

I am fluent in English and Spanish, which is the same language provided in **Part 4., Item Number 1.b.**, and I have read to this spouse beneficiary in the identified language every question and instruction on this form and his or her answer to every question. The spouse beneficiary informed me that he or she understands every instruction, question, and answer on the form, including the **Spouse Beneficiary's Certification**, and has verified the accuracy of every answer.

Interpreter's Signature

7.a. Interpreter's Signature [redacted]

7.b. Date of Signature (mm/dd/yyyy) 10/22/18

Part 6. Contact Information, Declaration, and Signature of the Person Preparing this Form, if Other Than the Spouse Beneficiary

Provide the following information about the preparer you used to complete Form I-130A if he or she is different from the preparer used to complete the Form I-130 filed on your behalf.

Preparer's Full Name

1.a. Preparer's Family Name (Last Name) [redacted]

1.b. Preparer's Given Name (First Name) [redacted]

2. Preparer's Business or Organization Name (if any) Law Offices of Brian D. Lerner, APC

Preparer's Mailing Address

3.a. Street Number and Name 3233 E. Broadway

3.b. ☐ Apt. ☐ Ste. ☐ Flr.

3.c. City or Town Long Beach

3.d. State CA 3.e. ZIP Code 90803

3.f. Province

3.g. Postal Code

3.h. Country USA

Part 6. Contact Information, Declaration, and Signature of the Person Preparing this Form, if Other Than the Spouse Beneficiary (continued)

Preparer's Contact Information

4. Preparer's Daytime Telephone Number

5. Preparer's Mobile Telephone Number (if any)

6. Preparer's Email Address (if any)

Preparer's Statement

7.a. ☐ I am not an attorney or accredited representative but have prepared this form on behalf of the spouse beneficiary and with the spouse beneficiary's consent.

7.b. ☒ I am an attorney or accredited representative and my representation of the spouse beneficiary in this case ☒ extends ☐ does not extend beyond the preparation of this form.

NOTE: If you are an attorney or accredited representative whose representation extends beyond preparation of this form, you may be obliged to submit a completed Form G-28, Notice of Entry of Appearance as Attorney or Accredited Representative, with this form.

Preparer's Certification

By my signature, I certify, under penalty of perjury, that I prepared this form at the request of the spouse beneficiary. The spouse beneficiary then reviewed this completed form and informed me that he or she understands all of the information contained in, and submitted with, his or her form, including the **Spouse Beneficiary's Certification,** and that all of this information is complete, true, and correct. I completed this form based only on information that the spouse beneficiary provided to me or authorized me to obtain or use.

Preparer's Signature

8.a. Preparer's Signature

8.b. Date of Signature (mm/dd/yyyy) 10/22/18

Part 7. Additional Information

If you need extra space to provide any additional information within this form, use the space below. If you need more space than what is provided, you may make copies of this page to complete and file with this form or attach a separate sheet of paper. Type or print your name and A-Number (if any) at the top of each sheet; indicate the **Page Number**, **Part Number**, and **Item Number** to which your answer refers; and sign and date each sheet.

1.a. Family Name (Last Name) [redacted]

1.b. Given Name (First Name) [redacted]

1.c. Middle Name [redacted]

2. A-Number (if any) ► **A-**

3.a. Page Number **3.b.** Part Number **3.c.** Item Number

3.d.

4.a. Page Number **4.b.** Part Number **4.c.** Item Number

4.d.

5.a. Page Number **5.b.** Part Number **5.c.** Item Number

5.d.

6.a. Page Number **6.b.** Part Number **6.c.** Item Number

6.d.

7.a. Page Number **7.b.** Part Number **7.c.** Item Number

7.d.

EXHIBITS

EXHIBIT '1':

Copy of Petitioner's Birth Certificate with English Translation

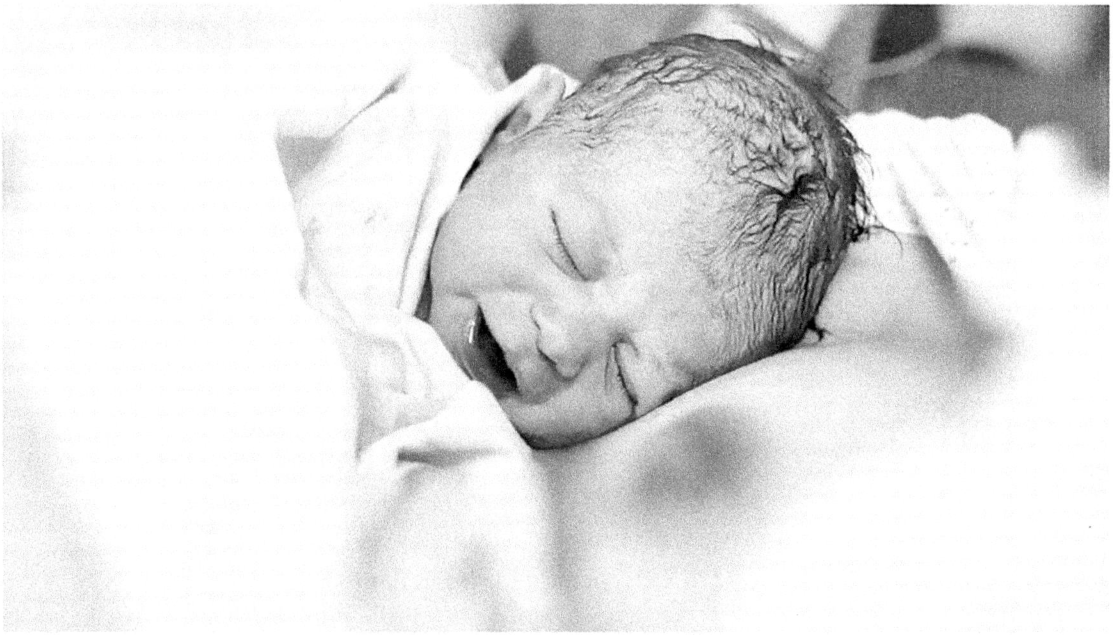

*** English Extract of Spanish Birth Certificate***
Civil Registration

Name of Registered Child:	
Sex:	Male
Date of Birth:	01/19/1965
Place of Birth:	Jaltepec, Tulancingo, Hidalgo, Mexico
Father of Child:	
Nationality:	Mexican
Age:	------- yrs.
Mother of Child:	
Nationality:	Mexican
Age	-------- yrs.

Certificate Information

Registration Date:	02/17/1965
Place of Issue:	Acatlan, Hidalgo, Mexico
Magistrate:	Alfredo Arciniega Olvera
Record Location:	Acatlan, Hidalgo, Mexico
Certificate:	No. 00080
Folio:	No. 21
Book:	No. 01

Translator's Certificate of Competence

I, certify that the above is an accurate translation of the original Birth Certificate in Spanish and that I am competent in both English and Spanish to render such translation.

9/27/18
Date

Law Offices of Brian D. Lerner
3233 East Broadway
Long Beach, CA 90803
Tel: (562) 495-0554

ACATLAN

2012 - 2016

Estado Libre y Soberano de Hidalgo

EN NOMBRE DEL ESTADO LIBRE Y SOBERANO DE HIDALGO Y COMO OFICIAL DEL REGISTRO DEL ESTADO FAMILIAR, HAGO SABER A LOS QUE LA PRESENTE VIEREN, Y CERTIFICO QUE EN EL LIBRO NUMERO 01 DEL REGISTRO QUE ES A MI CARGO, A LA FOJA 21 SE ENCUENTRAN ASENTADOS LOS DATOS SIGUIENTES:

ACTA DE NACIMIENTO

CRIP: --------
CURP: --------

OFICIALIA	LIBRO No.	ACTA No.	LOCALIDAD	FECHA DE REGISTRO
01	01	00080	ACATLAN	DIA MES AÑO 17/FEBRERO/1965

MUNICIPIO O DELEGACION	ENTIDAD FEDERATIVA
ACATLAN	HIDALGO

DATOS DEL REGISTRADO

NOMBRE(S)	PRIMER APELLIDO	SEGUNDO APELLIDO
[redacted]	[redacted]	[redacted]

NACIONALIDAD	SEXO
MEXICANA	MASCULINO

LUGAR Y FECHA DE NACIMIENTO

LOCALIDAD	MUNICIPIO	ENTIDAD	PAIS	FECHA
JALTEPEC	TULANCINGO	HIDALGO	MEXICO	19/ENERO/1965

COMPARECIO: EL PADRE

DATOS DE LOS PADRES

NOMBRE(S)	PRIMER APELLIDO	SEGUNDO APELLIDO
LEOBARDO	[redacted]	------------

NACIONALIDAD: MEXICANA

NOMBRE(S)	PRIMER APELLIDO	SEGUNDO APELLIDO
OFELIA	[redacted]	------------

NACIONALIDAD: MEXICANA

DATOS DE LOS ABUELOS

		NACIONALIDAD
ABUELO PATERNO:	------------	--------
ABUELA PATERNA:	------------	--------
ABUELO MATERNO:	------------	--------
ABUELA MATERNA:	------------	--------

LA PRESENTE ACTA CONTIENE ANOTACIONES AL REVERSO:

SE EXTIENDE ESTA CERTIFICACION EN CUMPLIMIENTO DEL ARTICULO 406 DE LA LEY PARA LA FAMILIA VIGENTE EN EL ESTADO DE HIDALGO, EN ACATLAN, HGO. EL SUSCRITO OFICIAL DEL REGISTRO DEL ESTADO FAMILIAR

REGISTRO DEL ESTADO FAMILIAR
ACATLAN, HGO.
2012 - 2016
SELLO DE LA OFICIALIA DEL REGISTRO DEL ESTADO FAMILIAR

LIC. ALFREDO ARCINIEGA OLVERA
OFICIAL DEL REGISTRO DEL ESTADO FAMILIAR

27/03/2013 13:27:25 4338084

EXHIBIT '2':
Copy of Petitioner's Legal Permanent Resident

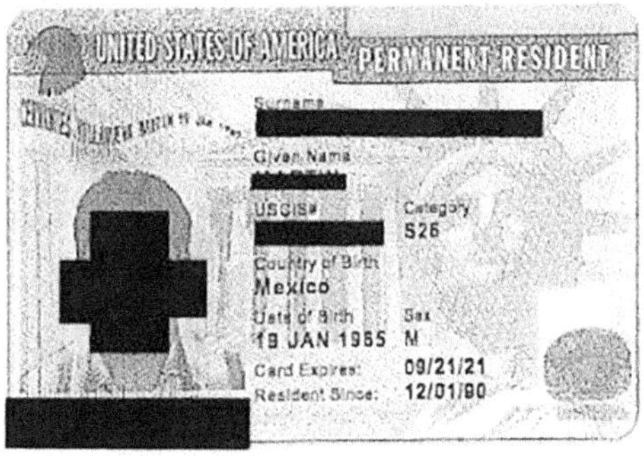
UNITED STATES OF AMERICA
PERMANENT RESIDENT
Surname
Given Name
USCIS#
Category
S26
Country of Birth
Mexico
Date of Birth
19 JAN 1965
Sex
M
Card Expires:
09/21/21
Resident Since:
12/01/90

6501196M2109217MEX<<<<<<<<<<<7

EXHIBIT '3':
Copy of Beneficiary's Birth Certificate with English Translation

***** English Extract of Spanish Birth Certificate*****
Civil Registration

Name of Registered Child:	[redacted]
Sex:	Female
Date of Birth:	01/03/1978
Place of Birth:	Tulpetlac, México City, Mexico
Father of Child:	[redacted]
Nationality:	Mexican
Age:	== yrs.
Mother of Child:	[redacted]
Nationality:	Mexican
Age	== yrs.

*****Certificate Information*****

Registration Date:	02/13/1978
Place of Issue:	Huasca de Ocampo, Hidalgo, Mexico
Magistrate:	Peralta-Hermosillo
Record Location:	Huasca de Ocampo, Hidalgo, Mexico
Certificate:	No. 00053
Folio:	No. 4702098
Book:	No. 01

Translator's Certificate of Competence

I, , certify that the above is an accurate translation of the original Birth C sh and that I am competent in both English and Spanish to render such translation.

10/22/18
Date

Law Offices of Brian D. Lerner
3233 East Broadway
Long Beach, CA 90803
Tel: (562) 495-0554

ESTADOS UNIDOS MEXICANOS

Estado Libre y Soberano de Hidalgo

EN NOMBRE DEL ESTADO LIBRE Y SOBERANO DE HIDALGO Y COMO DIRECTOR DEL REGISTRO DEL ESTADO FAMILIAR, HAGO SABER A LOS QUE LA PRESENTE VIEREN, Y CERTIFICO QUE EN EL LIBRO NUMERO 01 DEL REGISTRO QUE ES A MI CARGO, A LA FOJA 53 SE ENCUENTRAN ASENTADOS LOS DATOS SIGUIENTES:

ACTA DE NACIMIENTO

CRIP: ---------
CURP: ---------

OFICIALIA	LIBRO No.	ACTA No.	LOCALIDAD	FECHA DE REGISTRO
01	01	[redacted]	HUASCA DE OCAMPO	DIA MES AÑO 13/FEBRERO/1978

MUNICIPIO O DELEGACION	ENTIDAD FEDERATIVA
HUASCA DE OCAMPO	[redacted]

DATOS DEL REGISTRADO

[redacted]	[redacted]	PEREZ
NOMBRE(S)	PRIMER APELLIDO	SEGUNDO APELLIDO
MEXICANA	FEMENINO	
NACIONALIDAD	SEXO	

LUGAR Y FECHA DE NACIMIENTO

LOCALIDAD	MUNICIPIO	ENTIDAD	PAIS	FECHA
TULPETLAC	ECATEPEC DE MORELOS	MEXICO	MEXICO	03/ENERO/1978

COMPARECIO: EL PADRE

DATOS DE LOS PADRES

SANTIAGO	BARRON	CANO
NOMBRE(S)	PRIMER APELLIDO	SEGUNDO APELLIDO
MEXICANA		
NACIONALIDAD		
ANTONIA	PEREZ	DIMAS
NOMBRE(S)	PRIMER APELLIDO	SEGUNDO APELLIDO
MEXICANA		
NACIONALIDAD		

DATOS DE LOS ABUELOS

ABUELO PATERNO: [redacted] NACIONALIDAD: MEXICANA

ABUELA PATERNA: [redacted] NACIONALIDAD: MEXICANA

ABUELO MATERNO: [redacted] NACIONALIDAD: MEXICANA

ABUELA MATERNA: [redacted] NACIONALIDAD: MEXICANA

ESTADO DE HIDALGO

SE EXTIENDE ESTA CERTIFICACION EN CUMPLIMIENTO DEL ARTICULO 406 DE LA LEY PARA LA FAMILIA VIGENTE EN EL ESTADO DE HIDALGO, EN PACHUCA DE SOTO, HGO.

LIC. MARTÍN PERALTA HERMOSILLO
DIRECTOR DEL REGISTRO DEL ESTADO FAMILIAR

11/06/2014 12:11:26
FECHA DE EXPEDICION

SELLO DE LA DIRECCION DEL REGISTRO DEL ESTADO FAMILIAR

4702098

EXHIBIT '4':
Copy of Beneficiary's Foreign Passport

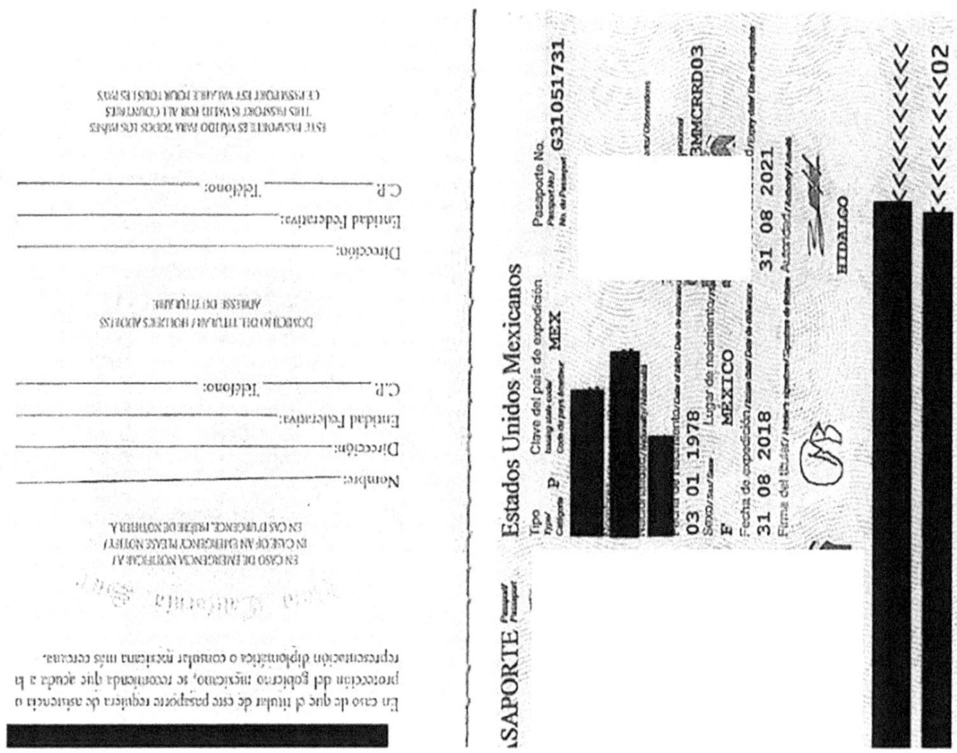

En caso de que el titular de este pasaporte requiera de asistencia o protección del gobierno mexicano, se recomienda que acuda a la representación diplomática o consular mexicana más cercana.

EN CASO DE EMERGENCIA NOTIFICAR A / IN CASE OF AN EMERGENCY PLEASE NOTIFY / EN CAS D'URGENCE, PRIÈRE DE NOTIFIER À

Nombre:
Dirección:
Entidad Federativa:
C.P. Teléfono:

DOMICILIO DEL TITULAR / HOLDER'S ADDRESS / ADRESSE DU TITULAIRE

Dirección:
Entidad Federativa:
C.P. Teléfono:

ESTE PASAPORTE ES VÁLIDO PARA TODOS LOS PAÍSES
THIS PASSPORT IS VALID FOR ALL COUNTRIES
CE PASSEPORT EST VALABLE POUR TOUS LES PAYS

PASAPORTE Passport
Estados Unidos Mexicanos
Tipo P
Clave del país de expedición MEX
Pasaporte No. G31051731
03 01 1978
Sexo F
Lugar de nacimiento MÉXICO
MMCRRD03
Fecha de expedición 31 08 2018
31 08 2021
HIDALGO
<<<<<<<<<<
<<<<<<<<02

EXHIBIT '5':

Copy of Petitioner and Beneficiary's Marriage Certificate

***** English Extract of Spanish Marriage Certificate*****
Civil Registration

Groom's Name:	[redacted] (Sex: Male)
Age:	30 years
Birth Place:	Jaltepec, Tulancingo, Hidalgo
Nationality:	Mexican
Father's Name:	
Nationality:	Mexican
Mother's Name:	
Nationality:	Mexican

Bride's Name:	[redacted] (Sex: Female)
Age:	18 years
Birth Place:	[redacted]
Nationality:	Mexican
Father's Name:	[redacted]
Nationality:	Mexican
Mother's Name:	[redacted]
Nationality:	Mexican

Certificate Information

Issue Date:	01/10/1996
Place of Issue:	[redacted]
Magistrate:	[illegible]
Record Location:	Book No. 1 / Certificate No. 04
Folio No.:	04

Translator's Certificate of Competence

I [redacted], certify that the above is an accurate translation of the original Marriage Certificate in Spanish and that I am competent in both English and Spanish to render such translation.

11/5/18
Date

Law Offices of Brian D. Lerner
3233 E. Broadway Avenue Long Beach, CA 90803

ESTADOS UNIDOS MEXICANOS

ESTADO LIBRE Y SOBERANO DE HIDALGO

REGISTRO DEL ESTADO FAMILIAR

No. DE CONTROL 145

EN NOMBRE DEL ESTADO LIBRE Y SOBERANO DE HIDALGO, Y COMO OFICIAL DEL REGISTRO DEL ESTADO FAMILIAR DE ESTE MUNICIPIO, C E R T I F I C O :
SER CIERTO QUE EN EL LIBRO NUM. UNO DEL AÑO 1996 DEL REGISTRO QUE ES A MI CARGO, EN LA FOJA NUMERO 04 SE ENCUENTRA ASENTADA EL ACTA NUM. 04 LEVANTADA POR EL OFICIAL DEL REGISTRO DEL ESTADO FAMILIAR ______ 10 DE ENERO DE 1996.
(LUGAR Y FECHA)
LA CUAL CONTIENE LOS SIGUIENTES DATOS:

ACTA DE MATRIMONIO

CONTRAYENTES

NOMBRE DEL CONTRAYENTE ______ EDAD 30
LUGAR DE NACIMIENTO ______ NACIONALIDAD MEXICANA
NOMBRE DE LA CONTRAYENTE ______ EDAD 18
LUGAR DE NACIMIENTO TULPETLAC, ESTADO DE MEXICO. NACIONALIDAD MEXICANA

PADRES DEL CONTRAYENTE

NOMBRE DEL PADRE ______ NACIONALIDAD MEXICANA
NOMBRE DE LA MADRE ______ NACIONALIDAD MEXICANA

PADRES DE LA CONTRAYENTE

NOMBRE DEL PADRE ______ (FINADO) NACIONALIDAD MEXICANA
NOMBRE DE LA MADRE ______ NACIONALIDAD MEXICANA

TESTIGOS DE LOS CONTRAYENTES

NOMBRE ______ EDAD 31 NACIONALIDAD MEXICANA
NOMBRE ______ EDAD 60 NACIONALIDAD MEXICANA
NOMBRE ______ EDAD 41 NACIONALIDAD MEXICANA
NOMBRE ______ EDAD 32 NACIONALIDAD MEXICANA

NOMBRE(S) DE LAS PERSONA(S) QUE DA(N) SU CONSENTIMIENTO POR MINORIA DE EDAD DE (LOS) CONTRAYENTE(S):

AUTORIZACION DE LA SECRETARIA DE GOBERNACION EN EL CASO DE CONTRAYENTE(S) ESTRANJERO(S):

ESTE CONTRATO DE MATRIMONIO ESTA SUJETO AL REGIMEN DE:

SOCIEDAD CONYUGAL (X) SEPARACION DE BIENES ( )

SE EXTIENDE ESTA CERTIFICACION, EN CUMPLIMIENTO DEL ARTICULO 386 DEL CODIGO FAMILIAR VIGENTE EN EL ESTADO, EN ______ GRANDE, HIDALGO.
A LOS 11 DIAS DEL MES DE ABRIL DE 2001.

SELLO DE LA OFICIALIA DEL REGISTRO DEL ESTADO FAMILIAR

EL C. OFICIAL DEL REGISTRO DEL ESTADO FAMILIAR, DOY FE

EXHIBIT '6':
Family Photos of Petitioner and Beneficiary

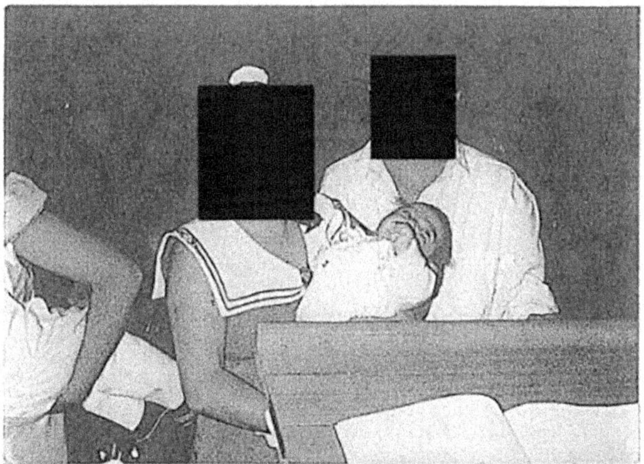

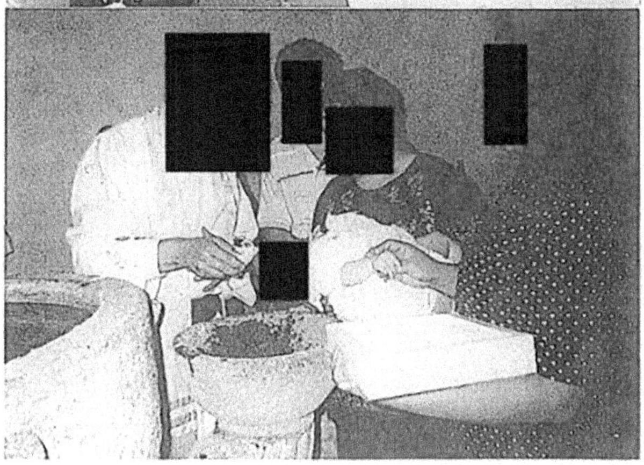

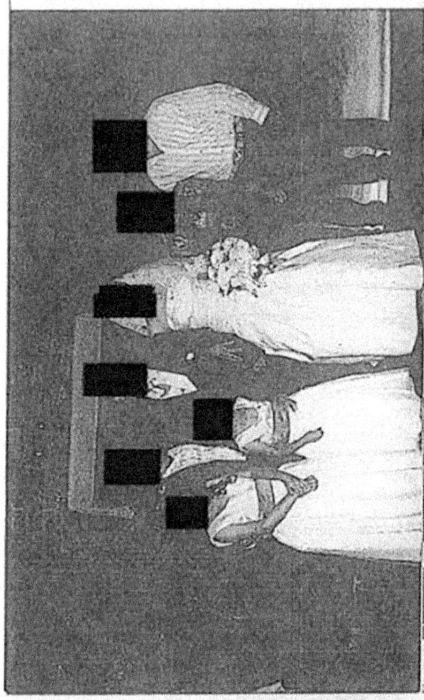

JESÚS ES LA PUERTA

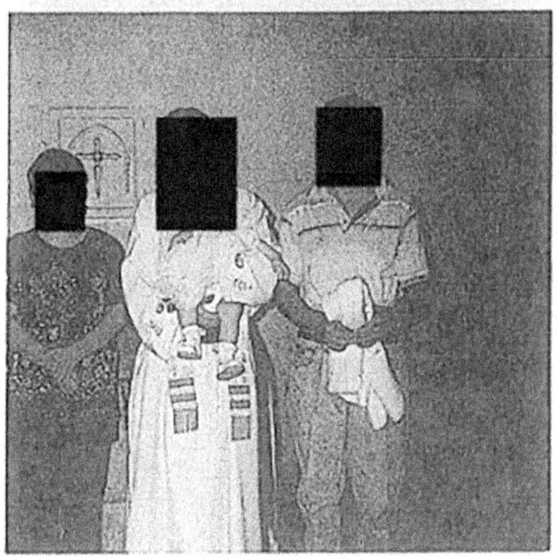

EXHIBIT '7':

Proof of Relationship between the Petitioner and the Beneficiary

*** English Extract of Spanish Birth Certificate***
Civil Registration

Name of Registered Child:	[redacted]
Sex:	Male
Date of Birth:	06/16/1997
Place of Birth:	Atotonilco el Grande, Hidalgo, Mexico
Father of Child:	[redacted]
Nationality:	Mexican
Age:	------- yrs.
Mother of Child:	[redacted]
Nationality:	Mexican
Age	-------- yrs.

Certificate Information

Registration Date:	08/29/1997
Place of Issue:	Atotonilco el Grande, Hidalgo, Mexico
Magistrate:	[redacted]
Record Location:	Atotonilco el Grande, Hidalgo, Mexico
Certificate:	No. 00490
Folio:	No. 490
Book:	No. 03

Translator's Certificate of Competence

I, [redacted], certify that the above is an accurate translation of the original Birth Certificate in Spanish and that I am competent in both English and Spanish to render such translation.

9/27/18
Date

Law Offices of Brian D. Lerner
3233 East Broadway
Long Beach, CA 90803
Tel: (562) 495-0554

Atotonilco
el Grande

Estado Libre y Soberano
de Hidalgo

EN NOMBRE DEL ESTADO LIBRE Y SOBERANO DE HIDALGO Y COMO OFICIAL DEL REGISTRO DEL ESTADO FAMILIAR, HAGO SABER A LOS QUE LA PRESENTE VIEREN, Y CERTIFICO QUE EN EL LIBRO NUMERO 03 DEL REGISTRO QUE ES A MI CARGO, A LA FOJA 490 SE ENCUENTRAN ASENTADOS LOS DATOS SIGUIENTES:

ACTA DE NACIMIENTO

CRIP:
CURP:

OFICIALIA	LIBRO No.	ACTA No.	LOCALIDAD	FECHA DE REGISTRO
				DIA MES AÑO
01	03	00490		29/AGOSTO/1997

MUNICIPIO O DELEGACION	ENTIDAD FEDERATIVA
	HIDALGO

DATOS DEL REGISTRADO

JOSE MARTIN		BARRON
NOMBRE(S)	PRIMER APELLIDO	SEGUNDO APELLIDO
MEXICANA	MASCULINO	
NACIONALIDAD	SEXO	

LUGAR Y FECHA DE NACIMIENTO

LOCALIDAD	MUNICIPIO	ENTIDAD	PAIS	FECHA
ATOTONILCO EL GRANDE	ATOTONILCO EL GRANDE	HIDALGO	MEXICO	16/JUNIO/1997

COMPARECIO: AMBOS

DATOS DE LOS PADRES

		VILLANUEVA
NOMBRE(S)	PRIMER APELLIDO	SEGUNDO APELLIDO
MEXICANA		
NACIONALIDAD		
	BARRON	PEREZ
NOMBRE(S)	PRIMER APELLIDO	SEGUNDO APELLIDO
MEXICANA		
NACIONALIDAD		

DATOS DE LOS ABUELOS

ABUELO PATERNO:	(FINADO)	NACIONALIDAD:	MEXICANA
ABUELA PATERNA:		NACIONALIDAD:	MEXICANA
ABUELO MATERNO:		NACIONALIDAD:	MEXICANA
ABUELA MATERNA:		NACIONALIDAD:	MEXICANA

SE EXTIENDE ESTA CERTIFICACION EN CUMPLIMIENTO DEL ARTICULO 406 DE LA LEY PARA LA FAMILIA VIGENTE EN EL ESTADO DE HIDALGO, EN ATOTONILCO EL GRANDE, HGO. EL SUSCRITO OFICIAL DEL REGISTRO DEL ESTADO FAMILIAR

REGISTRO DEL ESTADO FAMILIAR
MPIO. ATOTONILCO EL GRANDE, HGO.

2012 - 2016

SELLO DE LA OFICIALIA DEL REGISTRO DEL ESTADO FAMILIAR

OFICIAL DEL REGISTRO DEL ESTADO FAMILIAR

26/11/2014 10:22:29
FECHA DE EXPEDICION

5365459

*** English Extract of Spanish Birth Certificate***
Civil Registration

Name of Registered Child:	
Sex:	Female
Date of Birth:	12/18/2002
Place of Birth:	Tulancingo, Hidalgo, Mexico
Father of Child:	
Nationality:	Mexican
Age:	------- yrs.
Mother of Child:	
Nationality:	Mexican
Age	-------- yrs.

Certificate Information

Registration Date:	02/19/2003
Place of Issue:	Huasca de Ocampo, Hidalgo, Mexico
Magistrate:	
Record Location:	Huasca de Ocampo, Hidalgo, Mexico
Certificate:	No. 00075
Folio:	
Book:	No. 01

Translator's Certificate of Competence

I , certify that the above is an accurate translation of the original Birth Certificate in Spanish and that I am competent in both English and Spanish to render such translation.

10/22/18
Date

Law Offices of Brian D. Lerner
3233 East Broadway
Long Beach, CA 90803
Tel: (562) 495-0554

ESTADOS UNIDOS MEXICANOS

Gobierno Municipal
2012 - 2016
Huasca de Ocampo

Estado Libre y Soberano de Hidalgo

EN NOMBRE DEL ESTADO LIBRE Y SOBERANO DE HIDALGO Y COMO OFICIAL DEL REGISTRO DEL ESTADO FAMILIAR, HAGO SABER A LOS QUE LA PRESENTE VIEREN, Y CERTIFICO QUE EN EL LIBRO NUMERO 01 DEL REGISTRO QUE ES A MI CARGO, A LA FOJA 75 SE ENCUENTRAN ASENTADOS LOS DATOS SIGUIENTES

ACTA DE NACIMIENTO

CRIP:
CURP:

OFICIALIA	LIBRO No.	ACTA No.	LOCALIDAD	FECHA DE REGISTRO DIA MES AÑO
01	01	00075	HUASCA DE OCAMPO	19/FEBRERO/2003

MUNICIPIO O DELEGACION	ENTIDAD FEDERATIVA
HUASCA DE OCAMPO	HIDALGO

DATOS DEL REGISTRADO

DIANA		BARRON
NOMBRE(S)	PRIMER APELLIDO	SEGUNDO APELLIDO
MEXICANA	FEMENINO	
NACIONALIDAD	SEXO	

LUGAR Y FECHA DE NACIMIENTO

LOCALIDAD	MUNICIPIO	ENTIDAD	PAIS	FECHA
TULANCINGO	TULANCINGO		MEXICO	18/DICIEMBRE/2002

COMPARECIO: AMBOS

DATOS DE LOS PADRES

	CERVNATES	VILLANUEVA
NOMBRE(S)	PRIMER APELLIDO	SEGUNDO APELLIDO
MEXICANA		
NACIONALIDAD		
	BARRON	PEREZ
NOMBRE(S)	PRIMER APELLIDO	SEGUNDO APELLIDO
MEXICANA		
NACIONALIDAD		

DATOS DE LOS ABUELOS

ABUELO PATERNO:	NACIONALIDAD:	MEXICANA
ABUELA PATERNA: ...VA	NACIONALIDAD:	MEXICANA
ABUELO MATERNO:	NACIONALIDAD:	MEXICANA
ABUELA MATERNA:	NACIONALIDAD:	MEXICANA

SE EXTIENDE ESTA CERTIFICACION EN CUMPLIMIENTO DEL ARTICULO 406 DE LA LEY PARA LA FAMILIA VIGENTE EN EL ESTADO DE HIDALGO, EN HUASCA DE OCAMPO, HGO. EL SUSCRITO OFICIAL DEL REGISTRO DEL ESTADO FAMILIAR

REGISTRO DEL ESTADO FAMILIAR
MUNICIPIO DE HUASCA DE OCAMPO, HGO.

C. MARGARITA SOSA GUTIERREZ
OFICIAL DEL REGISTRO DEL ESTADO FAMILIAR

24/10/2013 09:11:08

*** English Extract of Spanish Birth Certificate***
Civil Registration

Name of Registered Child:	[redacted]
Sex:	Female
Date of Birth:	11/06/2001
Place of Birth:	Tulancingo, Hidalgo, Mexico
Father of Child:	[redacted]
Nationality:	Mexican
Age:	------- yrs.
Mother of Child:	[redacted]
Nationality:	Mexican
Age	-------- yrs.

Certificate Information

Registration Date:	02/18/2002
Place of Issue:	Huasca de Ocampo, Hidalgo, Mexico
Magistrate:	[redacted]
Record Location:	Huasca de Ocampo, Hidalgo, Mexico
Certificate:	[redacted]
Folio:	[redacted]
Book:	No. 01

Translator's Certificate of Competence

I, [redacted], certify that the above is an accurate translation of the original Birth Certificate in Spanish and that I am competent in both English and Spanish to render such translation.

10/22/18
Date

Law Offices of Brian D. Lerner
3233 East Broadway
Long Beach, CA 90803
Tel: (562) 495-0554

Gobierno Municipal
2012 - 2016
Huasca de Ocampo

Estado Libre y Soberano de Hidalgo

EN NOMBRE DEL ESTADO LIBRE Y SOBERANO DE HIDALGO Y COMO OFICIAL DEL REGISTRO DEL ESTADO FAMILIAR HAGO SABER A LOS QUE LA PRESENTE VIEREN, Y CERTIFICO QUE EN EL LIBRO NUMERO 01 DEL REGISTRO QUE ES A MI CARGO, A LA FOJA 55 SE ENCUENTRAN ASENTADOS LOS DATOS SIGUIENTES:

ACTA DE NACIMIENTO

CRIP: [redacted]
CURP: -

OFICIALIA	LIBRO No.	ACTA No.	LOCALIDAD	FECHA DE REGISTRO
01	01	[redacted]	HUASCA DE OCAMPO	DIA MES AÑO 18/FEBRERO/2002

MUNICIPIO O DELEGACION	ENTIDAD FEDERATIVA
HUASCA DE OCAMPO	HIDALGO

DATOS DEL REGISTRADO

NOMBRE(S)	PRIMER APELLIDO	SEGUNDO APELLIDO
ESMERALDA	CERVANTES	BARRON

NACIONALIDAD	SEXO
MEXICANA	FEMENINO

LUGAR Y FECHA DE NACIMIENTO

LOCALIDAD	MUNICIPIO	ENTIDAD	PAIS	FECHA
TULANCINGO	TULANCINGO	HIDALGO	MEXICO	06/NOVIEMBRE/2001

COMPARECIO: AMBOS

DATOS DE LOS PADRES

NOMBRE(S)	PRIMER APELLIDO	SEGUNDO APELLIDO
[redacted]	[redacted]	VILLANUEVA

NACIONALIDAD: MEXICANA

NOMBRE(S)	PRIMER APELLIDO	SEGUNDO APELLIDO
[redacted] GUADALUPE	BARRON	PEREZ

NACIONALIDAD: MEXICANA

DATOS DE LOS ABUELOS

ABUELO PATERNO: [redacted] NACIONALIDAD: MEXICANA

ABUELA PATERNA: [redacted] NACIONALIDAD: MEXICANA

ABUELO MATERNO: [redacted] NACIONALIDAD: MEXICANA

ABUELA MATERNA: [redacted] NACIONALIDAD: MEXICANA

SE EXTIENDE ESTA CERTIFICACION EN CUMPLIMIENTO DEL ARTICULO 405 DE LA LEY PARA LA FAMILIA VIGENTE EN EL ESTADO DE HIDALGO, EN HUASCA DE OCAMPO, HGO. EL SUSCRITO OFICIAL DEL REGISTRO DEL ESTADO FAMILIAR

REGISTRO DEL ESTADO FAMILIAR 2012 2016 MUNICIPIO DE HUASCA DE OCAMPO, HGO.
SELLO DE LA OFICIALIA DEL REGISTRO DEL ESTADO FAMILIAR

28/11/2014 10:44:46 5352706

Sigue Corporation
13291 Ralston Avenue
Sylmar, CA 91342

Cash Services
223 W 4TH ST
LOS ANGELES CA 90013
Fax: Tel: (213) 625-0067

ORDEN DE TRANSMISION (TRANSMISSION ORDER)

REMITENTE (SENDER)	BENEFICIARIO (BENEFICIARY)
(NAME, ADDRESS & PHONE) 10 LOS ANGELES, CA 90061	(NAME, ADDRESS & PHONE)
*** Numero De Cliente:	MEX Tel: NONE 6823 SIGUE VIAJES MONITUR RAYON # 102 B A 1 CUADRA DEL JARDIN PRINCIPAL

TRANSACCION (TRANSACTION)	DOLARES E.U (U.S Dollars)		TIPO DE CAMBIO (RATE OF EXCHANGE)
CANTIDAD NETA (NET BEFORE EXCHG)	460.00	12/20/08	13.24
COMISIONES (FEES)	10.00	AGENTE (AGENT) 14:51:19	MONEDA EXTRANJERA AL BENE (FOREIGN AMT TO BENE)
OTROS CARGOS (OTHER FEES)	0.00		
CANTIDAD TOTAL RECIBIDA (TOTAL AMOUNT RECEIVED)	470.00	FIRMA DEL REMITENTE (SENDER'S SIGNATURE)	

CURRENCY EXCHANGE: All payments will be made in local currency or in U.S Dollars, as applicable. Any difference between the exchange rate received by Sigue and the

COPIA DEL CLIENTE (CUSTOMER'S COPY)

Sigue Corporation
13291 Ralston Avenue
Sylmar, CA 91342

Agente (Agent)
Cash Services
223 W 4TH ST
LOS ANGELES CA 90013
Fax: (213) 625-0019 Tel: (213) 625-0067

ORDEN DE TRANSMISION (TRANSMISSION ORDER)

REMITENTE (SENDER)	BENEFICIARIO (BENEFICIARY)
(NAME, ADDRESS & PHONE) 10 LOS ANGELES, CA 90061	
*** Numero De Cliente: Infor: USA:1 800 385-3316	MEX Tel: NONE 6823 SIGUE VIAJES MONITUR RAYON # 102 B A 1 CUADRA DEL JARDIN PRINCIPAL
	11697

TRANSACCION (TRANSACTION)	DOLARES E.U (U.S Dollars)		TIPO DE CAMBIO (RATE OF EXCHANGE)
CANTIDAD NETA (NET BEFORE EXCHG)	500.00	02/27/09	15.17
COMISIONES (FEES)	10.00	AGENTE (AGENT)	MONEDA EXTRANJERA AL BENE (FOREIGN AMT TO BENE)
OTROS CARGOS (OTHER FEES)	0.00		
CANTIDAD TOTAL RECIBIDA (TOTAL AMOUNT RECEIVED)	510.00	FIRMA DEL REMITENTE (SENDER'S SIGNATURE)	7,585.00

CURRENCY EXCHANGE: All payments will be made in local currency or in U.S Dollars, as applicable. Any difference between the exchange rate received by Sigue and the exchange rate Sigue provides to its customers will be kept by Sigue, in addition to the transfer fees. Please ask the Agent for information ...

COPIA DEL CLIENTE (CUSTOMER'S COPY)

Sigue Corporation
13291 Ralston Avenue
Sylmar, CA 91342

Agente (Agent)
Cash Services
223 W 4TH ST
LOS ANGELES CA 90013
Fax: (213) 625-0019 Tel: (213) 625-0067

ORDEN DE TRANSMISION (TRANSMISSION ORDER)

REMITENTE (SENDER)	BENEFICIARIO (BENEFICIARY)
(NAME, ADDRESS & PHONE) A 2 10	(NAME, ADDRESS & PHONE)
*** Numero De Cliente: 1936296 Infor:	MEX Tel: NONE 6823 SIGUE VIAJES MONITUR RAYON # 102 B A 1 CUADRA DEL JARDIN PRINCIPAL
	11697

TRANSACCION (TRANSACTION)	DOLARES E.U (U.S Dollars)		TIPO DE CAMBIO (RATE OF EXCHANGE)
CANTIDAD NETA (NET BEFORE EXCHG)	450.00		

Sigue Corporation
13291 Ralston Avenue
Sylmar, CA 91342

Fax: (213) [redacted]-0019 Tel: (213) [redacted]067

REMITENTE (SENDER)	BENEFICIARIO (BENEFICIARY)
NOMBRE, DIRECCION Y TELEFONO (NAME, ADDRESS & PHONE)	NOMBRE Y DIRECCION (NAME & ADDRESS)
VILLANUEVA	BARRON PEREZ
224 W - 109TH ST	
	MEX Tel: NONE
*** Numero De Cliente: 1936296	1119 INTERMEX AGENTE PAGADOR CUAUHTEMOC
	CUAUHTEMOC N 114 COL CENTRO
	LUN - VIE 9:00 - 15:00 SAB 9:00 - 14:00 A UN COST

11697

TRANSACCION (TRANSACTION)			DOLARES E.U (U.S.Dollars)
CANTIDAD NETA (NET BEFORE EXCHG)			500.00
COMISIONES (FEES)			10.00
OTROS CARGOS (OTHER FEES) 0.00	Cargos del Estado (STATE FEE)	0.00	0.00
CANTIDAD TOTAL (TOTAL AMOUNT RECEIVED)			510.00

TIPO DE CAMBIO (RATE OF EXCHANGE): 12.94

MONEDA EXTRANJERA AL BENE (FOREIGN AMT TO BENE): 6,470.00

COPIA DEL CLIENTE (CUSTOMER'S COPY) ... in local currency or in U.S.Dollars, as applicable. Any difference between the exchange rate received by Sigue and the

Sigue Corporation
13291 Ralston Avenue
Sylmar, CA 91342

Agente (Agent)
Cash Services
223 W 4TH ST
LOS ANGELES CA 90013
Fax: (213) 625-0019 Tel: (213) 625-0067

ORDEN DE TRANSMISION (TRANSMISSION ORDER)

REMITENTE (SENDER)	BENEFICIARIO (BENEFICIARY)
NOMBRE, DIRECCION Y TELEFONO (NAME, ADDRESS & PHONE)	
W - 10	
(323) 240-4063	ATOTONILCO EL GRANDE
	HIDALGO
*** Numero De Cliente: 1936296	MEX Tel: NONE
	1119 INTERMEX AGENTE PAGADOR CUAUHTEMOC
Infor: USA:1 800 385-3316	CUAUHTEMOC N 114 COL CENTRO
	LUN - VIE 9:00 - 15:00 SAB 9:00 - 14:00 A UN COST

11697

TRANSACCION (TRANSACTION)			DOLARES E.U (U.S.Dollars)
CANTIDAD NETA (NET BEFORE EXCHG)			300.00
COMISIONES (FEES)			10.00
OTROS CARGOS (OTHER FEES) 0.00	Cargos del Estado (STATE FEE)	0.00	0.00
CANTIDAD TOTAL (TOTAL AMOUNT RECEIVED)			310.00

03/04/10

FIRMA DEL REMITENTE (SENDER'S SIGNATURE)

TIPO DE CAMBIO (RATE OF EXCHANGE): 12.83

MONEDA EXTRANJERA AL BENE (FOREIGN AMT TO BENE): 3,849.00

CURRENCY EXCHANGE: All payments will be made in local currency or in U.S.Dollars, as applicable. Any difference between the exchange rate received by Sigue and the exchange rate Sigue provides to its customers will be kept by Sigue. In addition to the transfer fees. Please ask the Agent for information ...

Sigue Corporation
13291 Ralston Avenue
Sylmar, CA 91342

Agente (Agent)
Cash Services
223 W 4TH ST
LOS ANGELES CA 90013
Fax: (213) 625-0019 Tel: (213) 625-0067

REMITENTE (SENDER)	BENEFICIARIO (BENEFICIARY)
NOMBRE, DIRECCION Y TELEFONO	NOMBRE Y DIRECCION (NAME & ADDRESS)
224 W - 1 9TH ST	
LOS ANGELES, CA 90061	ATOTONILCO EL GRANDE
	HIDALGO
*** Numero De Cliente: [redacted]	MEX Tel: NONE
	1119 INTERMEX AGENTE PAGADOR CUAUHTEMOC
	CUAUHTEMOC N 114 COL CENTRO
	LUN - VIE 9:00 - 15:00 SAB 9:00 - 14:00 A UN COST

11697

TRANSACCION (TRANSACTION)	DOLARES E.U (U.S.Dollars)
CANTIDAD NETA (NET BEFORE EXCHG)	1,000.00

TIPO DE CAMBIO (RATE OF EXCHANGE)

Sigue Corp.

Sigue Corporation
13291 Ralston Avenue
Sylmar, CA 91342

Cash Services
223 W 4TH ST
LOS ANGELES CA 90013
Fax: (213) 625-0019 Tel: (213) 625-0067

ORDEN DE TRANSMISION
(TRANSMISSION ORDER)

REMITENTE (SENDER)	BENEFICIARIO (BENEFICIARY)
NOMBRE, DIRECCION Y TELEFONO (NAME, ADDRESS & PHONE)	NOMBRE Y DIRECCION (NAME & ADDRESS)
224 W - 109TH ST LOS ANGELES, CA 90061 (323) 240-4063	ATOTONILCO EL GRANDE HIDALGO MEX Tel: NONE
*** Numero De Cliente:	1119 INTERMEX AGENTE PAGADOR CUAUHTEMOC CUAUHTEMOC N 114 COL CENTRO LUN - VIE 9:00 - 15:00 SAB 9:00 - 14:00 A UN COST

SI11697

TRANSACCION (TRANSACTION)				DOLARES E.U (U.S.Dollars)
CANTIDAD NETA (NET BEFORE EXCHG)				240.00
COMISIONES (FEES)				10.00
OTROS CARGOS (OTHER FEES)	0.00	Cargos del Estado (STATE FEE)	0.00	0.00
CANTIDAD TOTAL (TOTAL AMOUNT RECEIVED)				250.00

02/13/11

FIRMA DEL REMITENTE (SENDER'S SIGNATURE)

TIPO DE CAMBIO (RATE OF EXCHANGE): 12.20

MONEDA EXTRANJERA AL BENE (FOREIGN AMT TO BENE): 2,928.00

CURRENCY EXCHANGE: All payments will be made in local currency or in U.S.Dollars, as applicable. Any difference between the exchange rate received by Sigue and the

COPIA DEL CLIENTE (CUSTOMER'S COPY)

Sigue
MONEY TRANSFER SERVICES

Sigue Corporation
13291 Ralston Avenue
Sylmar, CA 91342

Agente (Agent)
Cash Services
223 W 4TH ST
LOS ANGELES CA 90013
Fax: (213) 625-0019 Tel: (213) 625-0067

ORDEN DE TRANSMISION
(TRANSMISSION ORDER)

REMITENTE NOMBRE, DIRECCION Y TEL (SENDER, NAME, ADDRESS & TEL)	BENEFICIARIO NOMBRE Y DIRECCION (BENEFICIARY NAME & ADDRESS)
224 W - 109TH ST LOS ANGELES, CA 90061	ATOTONILCO EL GRANDE HIDALGO MEX Tel: NONE
***Numero De Cliente: 1936296 Infor:	1119 (INT) INTERMEX CORRESPONSALES AGENTE PAGADOR CUAUHTEMOC N 114 COL CENTRO LUN - VIE 9:00 - 15:00 SAB 9:00 - 14:00 A un cos

SI11697

TRANSACCION (TRANSACTION)				DOLARES E.U (U.S.Dollars)
CANTIDAD NETA (NET BEFORE EXCHG)				500.00
COMISIONES (FEES)				10.00
OTROS CARGOS (OTHER FEES)	0.00	Cargos del Estado (STATE FEE)	0.00	0.00
CANTIDAD TOTAL (TOTAL AMOUNT RECEIVED)				510.00

FIRMA DEL REMITENTE (SENDER'S SIGNATURE)

TIPO DE CAMBIO (RATE OF EXCHANGE): 11.80

MONEDA EXTRANJERA AL BENE (FOREIGN AMT TO BENE): 5,900.00

CURRENCY EXCHANGE: All payments will be made in local currency or U.S. Dollars, as applicable. Any difference between the exchange rate received by Sigue and the exchange rate Sigue provides to its customers will be kept by Sigue, in addition to the transfer fees. Please ask the Agent for information concerning the currency exchange rate applicable to your transaction or call

Sigue
MONEY TRANSFER SERVICES

Sigue Corporation
13291 Ralston Avenue
Sylmar, CA 91342

Agente (Agent)
Cash Services
223 W 4TH ST
LOS ANGELES CA 90013
Fax: (213) 625-0019 Tel: (213) 625-0067

ORDEN DE TRANSMISION
(TRANSMISSION ORDER)

REMITENTE NOMBRE, DIRECCION Y TEL (SENDER, NAME, ADDRESS & TEL)	BENEFICIARIO NOMBRE Y DIRECCION (BENEFICIARY NAME & ADDRESS)
LOS ANGELES, CA 90061	ATOTONILCO EL GRANDE HIDALGO MEX Tel: NONE
*** Clave: 15274610627	5222 BANCOMER AV CUAUHTEMOC 317 JORGE VIESCA PALMA DEP CUENTA (ACCT DEP): 2796353673

SI11697

TRANSACCION (TRANSACTION)	DOLARES E.U (U.S.Dollars)
CANTIDAD NETA (NET BEFORE EXCHG)	500.00

TIPO DE CAMBIO (RATE OF EXCHANGE)

Sigue MONEY TRANSFER SERVICES

Sigue Corporation
13291 Ralston Avenue
Sylmar, CA 91342

Agente (Agent)
Cash Services
223 W 4TH ST
LOS ANGELES CA 90013
Fax: (213) 625-0019 Tel: (213) 625-0067

ORDEN DE TRANSMISION
(TRANSMISSION ORDER)

REMITENTE NOMBRE, DIRECCION Y TEL (SENDER, NAME, ADDRESS & TEL)	EFICIARY NAME & ADDRESS)
	ATOTONILCO EL GRANDE HIDALGO MEX Tel: NONE 5222 BANCOMER AV CUAUHTEMOC 317 JORGE VIESCA PALMA
***Numero De Cliente: Clave: 1 Infor: USA	DEP CUENTA (ACCT DEP):
	SI11697

TRANSACCION (TRANSACTION)			DOLARES E.U (U.S Dollars)
CANTIDAD NETA (NET BEFORE EXCHG)			600.00
COMISIONES (FEES)			10.00
OTROS CARGOS (OTHER FEES) 0.00	Cargos del Estado (STATE FEE)	0.00	0.00
CANTIDAD TOTAL (TOTAL AMOUNT RECEIVED)			610.00

AG

FIRMA DEL REMITENT

TIPO DE CAMBIO (RATE OF EXCHANGE) 12.95

MONEDA EXTRANJERA AL BENE (FOREIGN AMT TO BENE) 7,770.00

CURRENCY EXCHANGE: All payments will be made in local currency or U.S. Dollars, as applicable. Any difference between the exchange rate received by Sigue and the exchange rate Sigue provides to its customers will be kept by Sigue. In addition to the transfer fees. Please ask the agent for information concerning the currency exchange rate applicable to your transaction or call

Sigue MONEY TRANSFER SERVICES

Sigue Corporation
13291 Ralston Avenue
Sylmar, CA 91342

Agente (Agent)
Cash Services
223 W 4TH ST
LOS ANGELES CA 90013
Fax: (213) 625-0019 Tel: (213) 625-0067

ORDEN DE TRANSMISION
(TRANSMISSION ORDER)

REMITENTE ... SENDER, NAME, ADDRESS & TEL)	EFICIARY NAME & ADDRESS)
LOS ANGELES, CA 90061	DE OCAMPO HIDALGO ATOTONILCO EL GRANDE HIDALGO MEX Tel: NONE 5222 BANCOMER AV CUAUHTEMOC 317 JORGE VIESCA PALMA
***Numero De Cliente: 1936296 C 801 In r: USA:1 800 385-3 6	

Id Info: Document ID Estatal/State ID-A4762678 CA, USA 01/19/2017 SI11697

TRANSACCION (TRANSACTION)			DOLARES E.U (U.S Dollars)
CANTIDAD NETA (NET BEFORE EXCHG)			600.00
COMISIONES (FEES)			10.00
OTROS CARGOS (OTHER FEES) 0.00	Cargos del Estado (STATE FEE)	0.00	0.00
CANTIDAD TOTAL (TOTAL AMOUNT RECEIVED)			610.00

03/11/12

AGENTE (AGENT)

FIRMA DEL REMITENTE (SENDER'S SIGNATURE)

TIPO DE CAMBIO (RATE OF EXCHANGE) 12.80

MONEDA EXTRANJERA AL BENE (FOREIGN AMT TO BENE) 7,680.00

CURRENCY EXCHANGE: All payments will be made in local currency or U.S. Dollars, as applicable. Any difference between the exchange rate received by Sigue and the exchange rate Sigue

COPIA DEL CLIENTE (CUSTOMER'S COPY)

Sigue MONEY TRANSFER SERVICES

Sigue Corporation
13291 Ralston Avenue
Sylmar, CA 91342

Agente (Agent)
Cash Services
223 W 4TH ST
LOS ANGELES CA 90013
Fax: (213) 625-0019 Tel: (213) 625-0067

ORDEN DE TRANSMISION
(TRANSMISSION ORDER)

SENDER, NAME, ADDRESS & TEL)	EFICIARY NAME & ADDRESS)
	HIDALGO Tel: NONE
***Numero De Cliente: Cla	

Id Info: Document ID Estatal/State ID-A4762678 CA, USA 01/19/2017 SI11697

Sigue Corporation
13291 Ralston Avenue
Sylmar, CA 91342

Agente (Agent)
Sigue Los Angeles Branch #1
223 W 4th St
Los Angeles CA 90013
Fax: (213) 625-0019 Tel: (213) 625-5887

REMITENTE NOMBRE, DIRECCION Y TEL (SENDER, NAME, ADDRESS & TEL)	BENEFICIARIO NOMBRE Y DIRECCION (BENEFICIARY NAME & ADDRESS)
224 W - 109TH ST	DE OCAMPO HIDALGO ATOTONILCO EL GRANDE HIDALGO MEX Tel: NONE
***Numero De Cliente: 1936296 Clave:	

SI69100NC

TRANSACCION (TRANSACTION)	DOLARES E U (U.S Dollars)
CANTIDAD NETA (NET BEFORE EXCHG)	700.00
COMISIONES (FEES)	10.00
OTROS CARGOS (OTHER FEES) 0.00 / Cargos del Estado (STATE FEE) 0.00	0.00
CANTIDAD TOTAL (TOTAL AMOUNT RECEIVED)	710.00

NC

AGENTE (AGENT)

06/20/13 18:26:15 FECHA (DATE)

FIRMA DEL REMITENTE (SENDER'S SIGNATURE)

TIPO DE CAMBIO (RATE OF EXCHANGE) 13.35

MONEDA EXTRANJERA AL BENE (FOREIGN AMT TO BENE) 9,345.00

CURRENCY EXCHANGE: All payments will be made in local currency or U.S. Dollars, as applicable. Any difference between the exchange rate received b... of Agent / Fx... provides to its customers will be kept by Sigue, in addition to the transfer fees. Please ask the Agent for information concerning ... on rate Sigue

COPIA DEL CLIENTE / CUSTOMER'S COPY

Sigue Corporation
13291 Ralston Avenue
Sylmar, CA 91342

Agent / Agente
EBENEZER INTERNETY ASSESORES
724 S BROADWAY
LOS ANGELES CA 90014
Tel: (213) 688-4024 Fax: (213) 688-4024

California Department of Business Oversight (800) 622-0620 www.dfi.ca.gov

Sender / Remitente: (323) 240-4063
224 W 109TH ST
LOS ANGELES, CA 90061
SI69513

Customer number / Número de Cliente: 1936296 Date / Fecha: 12/20/13 14:51:28

Beneficiary/Beneficiario:	Payment Location / Lugar de Pago:
LOS CERRITOS, MUNICIPIO DE HUASCA DE OCAMPO HIDALGO ATOTONILCO EL GRANDE HIDALGO MEX Tel:	13006 TELEGRAFOS / ATOTONILCO, AVENIDA JORGE VIEZCA PALMA SIN NUMERO COL CENTRO,

Clave:

Transmission Order / Orden de Transmisión :

Transfer Amount / Monto a transferir	540.00
Transfer Fees / Comisiones	10.00
Other Fees / Otros Cargos	0.00
Taxes / Impuestos	0.00
Total Amount Received / Total a Recibir	550.00
Exchange Rate / Tipo de Cambio	13.00
Foreign Amount / Moneda Extranjera	7,020.00
Foreign Fee / Cargo Extranjero	0.00
Total to Beneficiary** / Total al Beneficiario**	7,020.00
Date Available* / Fecha Disponible*	12/21/2013

*I have read, understand and accept the terms of this contract / He leído, entendido y acepto los... este contrato.

Agent / Firma del Agente

*Funds are available during normal business hours of the paying location on or after the date indicated. Sender agrees that home delivery option may add additional day(s) to the indicated date. Los fondos están disponibles durante el horario normal de la ubicación de pago en o después de la fecha indicada. Remitente está de acuerdo en que la opción de entrega a domicilio puede agregar días adicionales a la fecha indicada. You have the right to dispute errors in your transaction. If you think there is an error, contact us within 180 days at 1(800) 385-3316 or via our website www.sigue.com. You can also contact us for a written explanation of your rights. You can cancel for a full refund within 30 minutes of payment, unless the funds have been picked up or deposited. Usted tiene el derecho a disputar errores

COPIA DEL CLIENTE / CUSTOMER'S COPY

Sigue Corporation
13291 Ralston Avenue
Sylmar, CA 91342

Agent / Agente
EBENEZER INTERNETY ASSESORES
-4024

California Department of Business Oversight (800) 622-0620 www.dfi.ca.gov

(323) 240-4063
224 W 109 TH ST
LOS ANGELES, CA 90061
SI69513

Customer number / Número de Cliente: 1936298 Date / Fecha: 02/17/14 16:27:20

Beneficiary/Beneficiario:	Payment Location / Lugar de Pago:
ATOTONILCO EL GRANDE HIDALGO MEX Tel:	13006 TELEGRAFOS / ATOTONILCO, AVENIDA JORGE VIEZCA PALMA SIN NUMERO COL CENTRO.

Clave:

Transfer Amount / Monto a transferir	550.00
Transfer Fees / Comisiones	10.00
Other Fees / Otros Cargos	0.00
Taxes / Impuestos	0.00
Total Amount Received / Total a Recibir	560.00
Exchange Rate / Tipo de Cambio	13.20
Foreign Amount / Moneda Extranjera	7,260.00
Foreign Fee / Cargo Extranjero	0.00

Sigue MONEY TRANSFER SERVICES

Sigue Corporation
13291 Ralston Avenue
Sylmar, CA 91342

EBENEZER INTERNETY ASSESORES
724 S BROADWAY
LOS ANGELES CA 90014
Tel: (213) 688-4024 Fax: (213) 688-4024

California Department of Business Oversight (800) 622-0620 www.dfi.ca.gov

Customer number / Número de Cliente: 1936298	Date / Fecha: 03/03/14 16:00:16
Beneficiary/Beneficiario: [redacted] ATOTONILCO EL GRANDE HIDALGO MEX Tel:	Payment Location / Lugar de Pago: 13006 TELEGRAFOS / ATOTONILCO, AVENIDA JORGE VIEZCA PALMA SIN NUMERO COL CENTRO
Clave: [redacted]	Infor: USA:1 800 385-3316
Transmission Order / Orden de Transmisión: [redacted]	

Sender / Remitente: [redacted] LOS ANGELES, CA 90061 (323) 240-4063 S169513

Transfer Amount / Monto a transferir	540.00
Transfer Fees / Comisiones	10.00
Other Fees / Otros Cargos	0.00
Taxes / Impuestos	0.00
Total Amount Received / Total a Recibir	550.00
Exchange Rate / Tipo de Cambio	13.30
Foreign Amount / Moneda Extranjera	7,182.00
Foreign Fee / Cargo Extranjero	0.00
Total to Beneficiary** / Total al Beneficiario**	7,182.00
Date Available* / Fecha Disponible*	3/4/2014

* I have read, understand and accept the terms of this contract / He leído, entendido y acepto los términos de este contrato.

Signature of Sender / Firma del Remitente Signature of Agent / Firma del Agente

*Funds are available during normal business hours of the paying location on or after the date indicated. Sender agrees that home delivery option may add additional day (s) to the indicated date. Los fondos están disponibles durante el horario normal de la ubicación de pago en o después de la fecha indicada. Remitente está de acuerdo en que la opción de entrega a domicilio puede agregar días adicionales a la fecha indicada. You have the right to dispute errors in your transaction. If you think there is an error, contact us within 180 days at 1(800) 385-3316 or via our website www.sigue.com. You can also contact us for a written explanation of your rights. You can cancel for a full refund within 30 minutes of payment, unless the funds have been picked up or deposited. Usted tiene el derecho a disputar errores en la transacción. Si usted cree que hay un error, póngase en contacto con nosotros dentro de los 180 días en el 1(800)385-3316 o en el sitio web www.sigue.com. También puede contactarnos para obtener una explicación por escrito de sus derechos. Puede cancelar la transacción dentro de los siguientes 30 minutos posteriores al pago y obtener un reembolso completo, a menos que los fondos hayan sido recogidos o depositados. For questions or complaints about Sigue Corporation contact / Para preguntas o quejas de Sigue contacte: 1(800) 385-3316 www.sigue.com. Consumer Financial Protection Bureau at 1(855) 411-2372 or www.consumerfinance.gov or contact the state agency indicated above / o contacte a la agencia estatal indicada en la parte superior. In the event you provide an incorrect account number or recipient institution

** Recipient may receive less due to taxes and additional non covered third party fees charged within destination country / Destinatario puede recibir una cantidad inferior debido impuestos cobrados en el país de destino

---

GOLDEN MONEY TRANSFER

517 4th Avenue, Suite 103, San Diego, CA 92101
Tel: (619) 702-5600 • Fax: 1-800-684-9645
Toll Free: 1-888-702-5656
CA License # 2401

Agent/Agente: THE GLAMOURAMA HAIRSTYLING
Address/Dirección: 10816 VALLEY MALL
City/State / Ciudad/Estado: EL MONTE / CA
Zip /C.P.: 91731
Tel.: 626-444-7478 Fax: 626-444-7478 ID: CA5053

Bank Reference # / Clave: [redacted]

Beneficiary / Beneficiario
Name / Nombre: [redacted] BARRON PEREZ
City/State / Ciudad/Estado: PACHUCA / HIDALGO
Tel. / Teléfono: /

Sender / Remitente Sender No. / Núm. de Remitente 331612
Address / Dirección: [redacted] ARMSTEAD ST
City/State / Ciudad/Estado: Azusa US-CA 91702 Zip / C.P.: 91702
Tel. / Teléfono: / 6268487124

Transaction Info / Información de envío

Net Amount / Cantidad:	190.00	USD
Charges / Cargos:	10.00	
Bank Surcharge / Cargo del Banco:		
Other Charges / Otros Cargos:	0.00	
Total Amount / Cantidad Total:	200.00	
Exchange Rate / Tipo de Cambio:	16.68	
Amount to receive / Cantidad a Recibir:	3169.20	MXN
Wire Date / Fecha: 11/19/2015	Cashier / Cajero: Ortencia Torres	

Location of Payment / Punto de Pago
Country / País: MEXICO
Bank / Pagador: (MX)(BTS) BANCOMER - (BTS) BANCOMER
Bank account / Número de Cuenta: [redacted]
City/State / Ciudad/Estado: PACHUCA / HIDALGO
Address / Dirección: [redacted]
Tel. / Teléfono:
Transmission Order # / Núm. de Transmisión: [redacted]

specifications.
Non covered third party fees may result in a change of the total amount

RIGHT TO REFUND

You, the customer, are entitled to a refund of the money to be transmitted as the result of this agreement if Golden Money Transfer, Inc., does not forward the money received from you within 10 days of the date of its receipt, or does not give instructions committing an equivalent amount of money to the person designated by you within 10 days of the date of the receipt of the funds from you unless otherwise instructed by you. If your instructions as to when the moneys shall be forwarded or transmitted are not complied with and the money has not yet been forwarded or transmitted, you have a right to a refund of your money. If you want a refund, you must mail or deliver your written request to Golden Money Transfer, Inc., at 517 4th Avenue, Suite 103, San Diego, CA 92101. If you do not receive your refund, you may be entitled to your money back plus a penalty of up to $1,000 and attorney's fees pursuant to Section 2102 of the California Financial Code.

DERECHO DE REEMBOLSO

Usted, el cliente, tiene derecho al reembolso del dinero que será transmitido como el resultado de este acuerdo si Golden Money Transfer, Inc., no envía el dinero entregado por usted dentro de 10 dias de haberlo recibido, o no da instrucciones comprometiéndose a equivaler la cantidad de dinero a la persona designada por usted dentro de

cu

CUSTOMER COPY/COPIA DEL [illegible]

MoneyGram Payment Systems, Inc.
1550 Utica Ave S
Minneapolis, MN 55416
1(800)926 3400
www.moneygram.com

TIENDA MEXICO - #15 - [illegible]ONTE

[illegible] 154180[illegible]
Fecha: 11[illegible] [illegible] 12:31 PM

Inf[illegible]mation/
[illegible] del remitente
[illegible]ERVANTES
[illegible]TEAD
[illegible]702
[illegible]65980758

[illegible] Information/
In[illegible] del destinatario:
[illegible]VANTES BARRON

[illegible] Destino Es[illegible]rado:
[illegible]EXICO
10 Minute Service [illegible] 10 minutos [illegible]

[illegible] Phone Call/[illegible]
[illegible] 1-888-925-5346
0655162808

[illegible]ence #/
N.º de referencia 72522409

Date Available in Receive Country/
[illegible]cha disponible en país de desti 11/22/2016
May be available sooner/*Puede estar disponible antes*

Transfer Amount/ Monto de la transferencia	4[illegible] USD
Transfer Fees/ Tarifa de la transferenci	+5.00 USD
Transfer Taxes/ transferencia:	+0.00 USD
Total/ Total:	54.12 USD
Exchange Rate/ Tipo de cambio:	1 USD = 20.3666 MXN
Transfer Amount/ transferencia:	1000.41 MXN
Other Fees/ Otras tarifas:	-0.00 MXN
Other Taxes/ Otros impuestos:	-0.00 MXN
Total to Recipient/ destinatario:	1000.41 MXN

Recipient may receive less due to fee[illegible] charged by the recipient's bank and foreign taxes./El recipiente puede recibir menos debido a honorarios cobrados [illegible] del recipiente e impuestos extranjeros.

You have a right to dispute errors in your transaction. If you think there is an error, contact us within 180 days at 1(800)926-9400 or www.moneygram.com. You can also contact us for a written explanation of your rights./Tiene derecho a reclamar los errores que encuentre en su transacción. Si cree que existe un error, comuníquese con nosotros en un plazo de 180 días

Client's Copy / Copia del Cliente

Ria
Continental Exchange Solutions, Inc.
dba Ria Financial Services
7001 Village Drive, Suite 200
Buena Park, CA. 90621, US
Tel: 1(800) 500-3994
Fax: 1(800) 281-7795

Tienda Chilango, LLC (CA6247)
Tienda Chilango, LLC (CA6247)
524 Stevens Ave
1
Solana Beach, CA 92075
Tel: (858) 523-0043
Fax: (858) 523-0118

Order No. / No. Orden [redacted]
PIN No. / Clave [redacted]

Transaction Date / Fecha de Transferencia 8/23/2016 6:05:50 PM

Track your Order at / Revise el estado de su orden en / www.riafinancial.com/global/track-a-transfer

Operator / Operador Isabel R
Date Available / Fecha Disponible: 8/29/2016
(May be available sooner / Puede estar disponible antes del tiempo estimado)

SENDER / CLIENTE
Customer No / No. Cliente [redacted]
714 N Sloan Ave, Compton
California 90221, United States
1-626 5980758

Transfer Amount / Monto	500.00	USD
Transfer Fees / Cargos	10.00	USD
Transfer Taxes / Impuestos	0.00	USD
Total	**510.00**	**USD**

RECIPIENT / BENEFICIARIO

Exchange Rate / Tipo de Cambio
$ 1.00 USD = 18.17 MXN

Transfer Amount / Monto	9,085.00	MXN
Other Fees / Otros Cargos	0.00	MXN
Total to Recipient	9,085.00	MXN

PAYING AGENT / AGENTE PAGADOR
BBVA BANCOMER, S.A.
XXXXXXX98

Recipient may receive less due to fees charged by the recipient's bank and foreign taxes. / El Beneficiario puede recibir menos debido a cargos aplicados por el banco o país destino.

RIGHT TO REFUND: "You, the customer, are entitled to a refund of the money to be transmitted as a result of this agreement if Continental Exchange Solutions, Inc. dba Ria Financial Services ("RIA") does not forward the money received from you within 10 days of the date of its receipt, or does not give instructions

[illegible]

vigo

RECEIPT/RECIBO

Thank you/Gracias

TRACKING NUMBER (MTCN)/
NO. DE CONTROL DEL ENVIO:
973-239-1654

For customer service please call 1 800 777 8784/Para comunicarse con el servicio de atención al cliente, llame al 1 800 777 8784

My WOW #
Total Points/Puntos totales

DF RECORDS
6971 LINCOLN AVE STE C, CA

Money Transfer/Envío de Dinero
CASH/Dinero en efectivo

Operator ID/No. ID del Operador [illegible]

Date of Transaction/Fecha de Transacción
January 23, 2017/Enero 23, 2017

Time of Transaction/Hora de la Transacción
11:50 AM PST

Sender/Remitente
MARTIN CERVANTES VILLANUEVA
18331 E ARMSTEAD AZUSA CA 91702 USA
6265980758

Receiver/Destinatario
MARIA GUADALUPE BARRON PEREZ
ATOTONILCO EL GRANDE
PACHUCA
HIDALGO

7711511702

Bank Name/Nombre del Banco
Bancomer (10 or 16 digit account#)

Bank Account Number/No. de Cuenta Bancaria
*****9098

Expected Payout Location/
Localidad donde Esperan Pago

Client's Copy / Copia del Cliente

AFEX
Continental Exchange Solutions, Inc.
dba AFEX Money Express
7001 Village Drive, Suite 200
Buena Park, CA 90621
Tel : 1 (800) 500-3994
Fax : 1 (800) 281-7795

Df Records
Df Records (132233)

(714) 252-9224
6971 Lincoln Ave Buena Park, CA 90620

Order No. / No. Orden US1106488481

PIN No. / Clave 17634804542

Transaction Date / Fecha de Transferencia 12/16/2016 2:59 PM
Operator / Operador Helen C
Date Available / Fecha Disponible 12/21/2016
(May be available sooner / Puede estar disponible antes del tiempo estimado)

SENDER / CLI[illegible]
Customer No / [illegible] 769077093
LORENA CORN[illegible]
714 N Sloan A[illegible]
Compton, C[illegible] 9[illegible]
626 5980758

Transfer Amount / Monto	5[illegible]
Transfer Fees / [illegible]	1[illegible]
Transfer Taxes / Impuesto[illegible]	0.00 [illegible]
Total	**510.00 USD**

RECIPIENT / BENEFICIARIO
MARIA GUADALUPE BARRON PEREZ
ATOTONILCO EL GRANDE, HGO, MX

Exchange Rate / Tipo de Cambio
$1.00 USD = 20.31 MXN

Transfer Amount / Monto	10,155.00 MXN
Other Fees / Otros Cargos	0.00
Total to Recipient	**10,155.00 MXN**

PAYING AGENT / AGENTE PAGADOR
BANCOMER
2945409098
Cuenta de Ahorro

Recipient may receive less due to fees charged by the recipient's bank and foreign taxes. / El Beneficiario puede recibir menos debido a cargos aplicados por el banco o país destino.
RIGHT TO REFUND: "You, the customer, are entitled to a refund of the money to be transmitted as a result of this agreement if Continental Exchange Solutions, Inc. dba AFEX Money Express ("AFEX") does not forward the money received from you within 10 days of the date of its receipt, or does not give instructions committing an equivalent amount of money to the person designated by you within 10 days of the date of the receipt of the funds from you unless otherwise instructed by you. If your instructions as to when the money shall be forwarded or transmitted are not complied with and the money has not yet been forwarded or transmitted you have a right to a refund of your money. If you want a refund, you must mail or deliver your written request to AFEX at 7001 Village Drive, Suite 200 - Buena Park, CA 90621. If you do not receive your refund, you may be entitled to your money back plus a penalty of up to $1,000 and attorney's fees pursuant to Section 2102 of the California Financial Code."
CURRENCY EXCHANGE CHARGES: In the event that a sending customer requests payment to a beneficiary in

RECEIPT/RECIBO
Thank you/Gracias

TRACKING NUMBER (MTCN)/
NO. DE CONTROL DEL ENVIO:
973-229-6560

For Customer Service please call 1-800-777-8784/Para comunicarse con el servicio de atención al cliente llame al 1-800-777-8784

My WU® #
Total Points/Puntos totales

DE RECORDS
[illegible] LINCOLN AVE STE C, CA
7142529224

Money Transfer/Envío de Dinero
CASH/Dinero en efectivo

Operator ID/No. ID del Operador [illegible]

Date of Transaction/Fecha de Transacción
September 09, 2017/septiembre 09, 2017

Time of Transaction/Hora de la Transacción
02:20 PM PDT

Sender/Remitente
MARTIN CERVANTES VILLANUEVA
18331 E ARMSTEAD, AZUSA, CA 91702 USA
6265980768

R[illegible]er/Destinatario
[illegible] GUADALUPE BARRON PEREZ
A[illegible]ONILCO EL GRANDE
ATOTONILCO EL GRANDE
HIDALGO

7711511792

Bank Name/Nombre del Banco
Bancomer (10 or 16 digit account#)

Bank Account Number/No. de Cuenta Bancaria
*****9098

Expected Payout Location/

973-0786655

RECEIPT/RECIBO
Thank you/Gracias

$3,014.50

For Customer Service please call 1-800-777-8784/Para comunicarse con el servicio de atención al cliente llame al 1-800-777-8784

My WU® #
Total Points/Puntos totales

MULTISERVICE EL PAISITA
732 1/2 S BROADWAY, CA

Money Transfer/Envío de Dinero
CASH/Dinero en efectivo

Operator ID/No. ID del Operador 604

Date of Transaction/Fecha de Transacción
June 05, 2017/Junio 05, 2017

Time of Transaction/Hora de la Transacción
02:50 PM PDT

[illegible] Remitente
[illegible] CERVANTES VILLANUEVA
[illegible] ARMSTEAD, AZUSA, CA 91702 USA
6265980768

Receiver/Destinatario
MARIA GUADALUPE BARRON PEREZ
ATOTONILCO EL GRANDE
,ATOTONILCO EL GRANDE,
,HIDALGO

7711511792

Bank Name/Nombre del Banco
Bancomer (10 or 16 digit account#)

Bank Account Number/No. de Cuenta Bancaria
*****9098

Expected Payout Location/
Localidad donde Esperan Pago
ATOTONILCO EL GRANDE, HIDALGO
Mexico/México

Service Type/Tipo de Servicio
DIRECT TO BANK

RECEIPT/RECIBO

Thank you/Gracias

TRACKING NUMBER (MTCN)/
NO. DE CONTROL DEL ENVIO:
972-889-3017

For Customer Service, please call 1-800-777-8784/Para comunicarse con el servicio de atención al cliente, llame al 1-800-777-8784

My WU® #
Total Points/Puntos totales

ENVIOS SEGUROS CASTRO
10450 BEACH BLVD 101, CA
7148262761

Money Transfer/Envio de Dinero
CASH/Dinero en efectivo

Operator ID/No. ID del Operador: 006

Date of Transaction/Fecha de Transaccion
May 16, 2018/Mayo 16, 2018

Time of Transaction/Hora de la Transaccion
05:02 PM PDT

Sender/Remitente
[redacted] CERVANTES VILLANUEVA
18331 E ARMSTEAD, AZUSA, CA, 91702, USA
6265980758

Receiver/Destinatario
JOSE [redacted] CERVANTES BARRON

Expected Payout Location/
Localidad donde Esperan Pago
ATOTONILCO EL GRANDE, HIDALGO,
Mexico/México

Service Type/Tipo de Servicio
ELEKTRA CASH/DINERO EN EFECTIVO

Date Available in Receiver's Country/Fecha Disponible en el País del Destinatario
May 16, 2018/Mayo 16, 2018

Transfer Amount/ Cantidad de Envio:		50.00 USD
Transfer Fees/ Cargos por Envio	+	10.00 USD
Additional Fees/ Cargos Adicionales	+	0.00 USD
Transfer Taxes/	+	0.00 USD

RECEIPT/RECIBO

Thank you/Gracias

TRACKING NUMBER (MTCN)/
NO. DE CONTROL DEL ENVIO:
973-979-3530

For Customer Service, please call 1-800-777-8784/Para comunicarse con el servicio de atención al cliente, llame al 1-800-777-8784

My WU® #
Total Points/Puntos totales

DF RECORDS
6971 LINCOLN AVE STE C CA
7142620224

Money Transfer/Envio de Dinero
CASH/Dinero en efectivo

Operator ID/No. ID del Operador: KZ1

Date of Transaction/Fecha de Transaccion
March 30, 2018/Marzo 30, 2018

Time of Transaction/Hora de la Transacción
01:22 PM PDT

Sender/Remitente
[redacted] CERVANTES VILLANUEVA
18331 E ARMSTEAD, AZUSA, CA, 91702, USA
6265980758

Receiver/Destinatario
[redacted] BARRON PEREZ
ATOTONILCO EL GRANDE
ATOTONILCO EL GRANDE
HIDALGO

7711511792

Bank Name/Nombre del Banco
Bancomer (10 or 16 digit account#)

Bank Account Number/No. de Cuenta Bancaria
******9098

Expected Payout Location/
Localidad donde Esperan Pago
ATOTONILCO EL GRANDE, HIDALGO,
Mexico/Mexico

vigo MONEY TRANSFER

RECEIPT/RECIBO
Thank you/Gracias

TRACKING NUMBER (MTCN)/
NO. DE CONTROL DEL ENVIO:
973-129-0257

For Customer Service, please call 1-800-777-8784/Para comunicarse con el servicio de atencion al cliente, llame al 1-800-777-8784

DF RECORDS
6071 LINCOLN AVE STE C CA
7142529224

Money Transfer/Envio de Dinero
CASH/Dinero en efectivo

Operator ID/No. ID del Operador: 005

Date of Transaction/Fecha de Transaccion
September 28, 2018/Septiembre 28, 2018

Time of Transaction/Hora de la Transaccion
04:08 PM PDT

Remitente:
CERVANTES VILLANUEVA
ARMSTEAD, AZUSA, CA, 91702, USA
6265980758

er/Destinatario
GUADALUPE BARRON PEREZ
A TONILCO EL GRANDE
ATOTONILCO EL GRANDE
HIDALGO

7711511792

Bank Name/Nombre del Banco:
Bancomer (10 or 16 digit account#)

Bank Account Number/No. de Cuenta Bancaria:
******9098

Expected Payout Location/
Localidad donde Esperan Pago:
ATOTONILCO EL GRANDE, HIDALGO,
Mexico/México

Service Type/Tipo de Servicio:
DIRECT TO BANK/DIRECTO A BANCO

intermex
International Money Express
Inter x Wire Transfer, Corp
9480 S. Dixie Hwy
Miami, FL 33156
1-877-999-0190
MI ENVIO IN C & A
Telefono/Phone: (714) 826-2761
10450 BEACH BLVD STE 101
STANTON, CALIFORNIA 90680
CA-1829
GIRO/WIRE:CA-1829-119614
06/19/2018 03:59 pm PST
REMITENTE/SENDER
VILLANUEVA
18331 E ARMSTEAD
STANTON CALIFORNIA90680
Telefono:
BENEFICIARIO/BENEFICIARY
BARRON
PEREZ

Telefono/Phone: 000
Pais/Country: MEXICO
PUNTO DE PAGO/ Payment at:
Pagador/Payer: BANCOMER
Ciudad/City:
Estado/State:
Cuenta/Acc No.: 2945409098
Banco/Bank: BANCOMER
TRANSFERENCIA / WIRE

Monto / Transfer Amount	$650.00
Transfer Fees paid in cash / Cargos de Transferencia en Cash	$10.00
Otros/Other chg	$0.00
Estado Cargos/Transfer Taxes:	$0.00
Descuento/Discount:	$0.00
Total a pagar / Total due	**$660.00**
Tipo de Cambio Exchange Rate:	20.5400
Monto a entregar Total to Recipient	13,351.00 MXN

Servicio al Cliente / Customer Service
1-800-670-8611
Disponible/Available 6/20/2018

X

Firma del Cliente
RECLAME SU GIRO COMO GIRO

RECEIPT/RECIBO

Thank you/Gracias

TRACKING NUMBER (MTCN)/
NO. DE CONTROL DEL ENVIO:
973-306-4241

For Customer Service, please call 1-800-777-8784/Para comunicarse con el servicio de atención al cliente, llame al 1-800-777-8784

DF RECORDS
6971 LINCOLN AVE STE C, CA
7142529224

Money Transfer/Envio de Dinero
CASH/Dinero en efectivo

Operator ID/No. ID del Operador 005

Date of Transaction/Fecha de Transacción
October 09, 2018/Octubre 09, 2018

Time of Transaction/Hora de la Transacción:
04.33 PM PDT

Sender/Remitente
[redacted] CERVANTES VILLANUEVA
18331 E ARMSTEAD, AZUSA, CA, 91702, USA
6265980768/ 264

Receiver/Destinatario
[redacted] BARRON PEREZ
ATOTONILCO EL GRANDE
,ATOTONILCO EL GRANDE
,HIDALGO

7711511792

Bank Name/Nombre del Banco
Bancomer (10 or 16 digit account#)

Bank Account Number/No. de Cuenta Bancaria
******0098

Expected Payout Location/
Localidad donde Esperan Pago
ATOTONILCO EL GRANDE, HIDALGO,
Mexico/México

Service Type/Tipo de Servicio
DIRECT TO BANK/DIRECTO A BANCO

ABOUT THE AUTHOR

Brian D. Lerner is an Immigration Lawyer and runs a National Immigration Law Firm for nearly 30 years. He is an attorney who is a certified specialist that might help in Immigration & Nationality Law as issued by the California State Bar, Board of Legal Specialization. Attorney Lerner is an expert in Immigration Law, Removal and Deportation, Citizenship, Waiver and Appeals.

He has been a licensed attorney since 1992 and started the Law Offices of Brian D. Lerner, APC. The immigration practice consists of Immigration and Nationality Law, and everything involved with and regarding immigration which includes citizenship, investment visas, family and employment visas, removal and deportation hearings, appeals, waivers, adjustment, consulate processing and all types of immigration and citizenship matters.

He has represented clients from all over the U.S. and in many countries around the world. One side of his practice is dedicated to keeping people in the U.S. and fighting for their immigration rights, while another side is to get people back who have been deported and removed from the U.S.

Also, there is the affirmative part of Immigration Law which Brian Lerner has helped numerous people come into the U.S. on business visas, investment visas, student visas, fiancée and marriage visas, religious visas and many more. Attorney Lerner has helped immigrants who are victims of crime and domestic violence or ones that are married to abusers.

In other words, Attorney Lerner has a firm that helps people all over the U.S. He has dedicated significant time to preparing numerous petitions and applications for you to get at a fraction of the price of hiring an attorney. He says it is the next best thing to a real attorney because they are real petitions prepared by an expert.

www.ingramcontent.com/pod-product-compliance
Lightning Source LLC
Chambersburg PA
CBHW061356240926
51846CB00007B/1431